Microsoft® Windows 7

ILLUSTRATED

Essentials

Barbara Clemens

COURSE TECHNOLOGY
CENGAGE Learning·

Australia · Brazil · Japan · Korea · Mexico · Singapore · Spain · United Kingdom · United States

COURSE TECHNOLOGY
CENGAGE Learning™

Microsoft® Windows® 7—Illustrated Essentials
Barbara Clemens

Executive Editor: Marjorie Hunt

Associate Acquisitions Editor: Brandi Shailer

Senior Product Manager: Christina Kling Garrett

Associate Product Manager: Michelle Camisa

Editorial Assistant: Kim Klasner

Director of Marketing: Cheryl Costantini

Senior Marketing Manager: Ryan DeGrote

Marketing Coordinator: Kristen Panciocco

Developmental Editor: Rachel Biheller Bunin

Senior Content Project Manager: Catherine G. DiMassa

Copyeditor: Mark Goodin

Proofreader: Debbie Masi

Indexer: Alexandra Nickerson

QA Manuscript Reviewers: Serge Palladino, Jeff Schwartz

Cover Designer: GEX Publishing Services

Cover Artist: Mark Hunt

Composition: GEX Publishing Services

Photos pps. vii and page 28 courtesy of Shutterstock® Images LLC.

For product information and technology assistance, contact us at
Cengage Learning Customer & Sales Support, 1-800-354-9706

For permission to use material from this text or product, submit all requests online at **www.cengage.com/permissions**
Further permissions questions can be emailed to
permissionrequest@cengage.com

ISBN-13: 978-0-538-75077-6
ISBN-10: 0-538-75077-4

Course Technology
20 Channel Center Street
Boston, MA 02210
USA

Cengage Learning is a leading provider of customized learning solutions with office locations around the globe, including Singapore, the United Kingdom, Australia, Mexico, Brazil, and Japan. Locate your local office at:
international.cengage.com/region

Cengage Learning products are represented in Canada by Nelson Education, Ltd.

To learn more about Course Technology, visit **www.cengage.com/coursetechnology**

To learn more about Cengage Learning, visit **www.cengage.com.**

Purchase any of our products at your local college store or at our preferred online store
www.CengageBrain.com

Printed in the United States of America
2 3 4 5 6 7 8 9 12 11 10

Contents

Preface

Welcome to *Microsoft Windows 7—Illustrated Essentials*. If this is your first experience with the Illustrated series, you'll see that this book has a unique design: each skill is presented on two facing pages, with steps on the left and screens on the right. The layout makes it easy to learn a skill without having to read a lot of text and flip pages to see an illustration.

This book is an ideal learning tool for a wide range of learners—the "rookies" will find the clean design easy to follow and focused with only essential information presented, and the "hotshots" will appreciate being able to move quickly through the lessons to find the information they need without reading a lot of text. The design also makes this a great reference after the course is over! See the illustration on the right to learn more about the pedagogical and design elements of a typical lesson.

What's New in this Edition

- **Coverage**—This book features step-by-step instructions on essential skills including learning the Windows 7 desktop, managing windows, working with programs, and managing files and folders.

- **Projects set within case study**—Students explore important topics such as safe computer use, knowledge of their computer hardware devices, and appropriate file structures for given business situations.

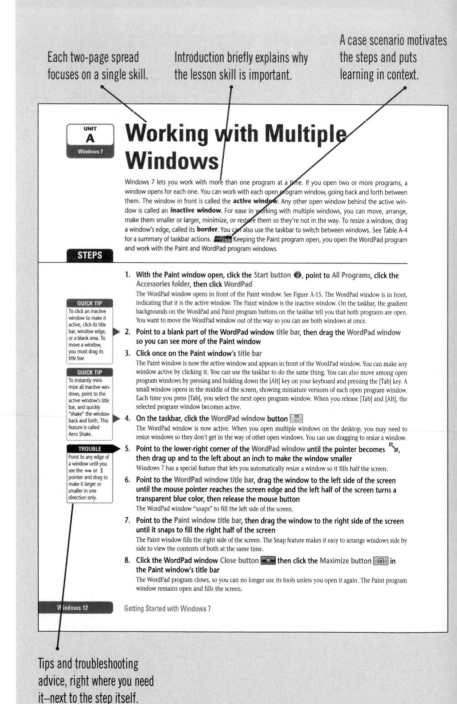

Each two-page spread focuses on a single skill.

Introduction briefly explains why the lesson skill is important.

A case scenario motivates the steps and puts learning in context.

Tips and troubleshooting advice, right where you need it–next to the step itself.

Large screen shots keep
students on track as
they complete steps.

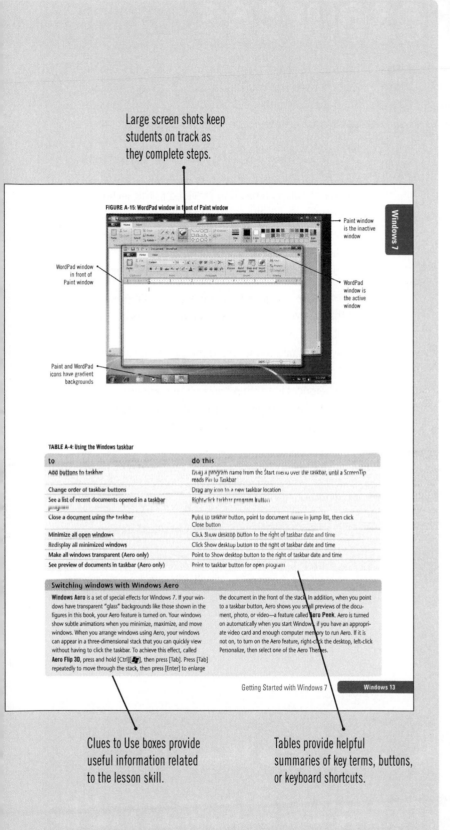

FIGURE A-15: WordPad window in front of Paint window

Paint window
is the inactive
window

WordPad window
in front of
Paint window

WordPad
window is
the active
window

Paint and WordPad
icons have gradient
backgrounds

TABLE A-4: Using the Windows taskbar

to	do this
Add buttons to taskbar	Drag a program name from the Start menu over the taskbar, until a ScreenTip reads Pin to Taskbar
Change order of taskbar buttons	Drag any icon to a new taskbar location
See a list of recent documents opened in a taskbar program	Right-click taskbar program button
Close a document using the taskbar	Point to taskbar button, point to document name in jump list, then click Close button
Minimize all open windows	Click Show desktop button to the right of taskbar date and time
Redisplay all minimized windows	Click Show desktop button to the right of taskbar date and time
Make all windows transparent (Aero only)	Point to Show desktop button to the right of taskbar date and time
See preview of documents in taskbar (Aero only)	Point to taskbar button for open program

Switching windows with Windows Aero

Windows Aero is a set of special effects for Windows 7. If your windows have transparent "glass" backgrounds like those shown in the figures in this book, your Aero feature is turned on. Your windows show subtle animations when you minimize, maximize, and move windows. When you arrange windows using Aero, your windows can appear in a three-dimensional stack that you can quickly view without having to click the taskbar. To achieve this effect, called **Aero Flip 3D**, press and hold [Ctrl][⊞], then press [Tab]. Press [Tab] repeatedly to move through the stack, then press [Enter] to enlarge the document in the front of the stack. In addition, when you point to a taskbar button, Aero shows you small previews of the document, photo, or video—a feature called **Aero Peek**. Aero is turned on automatically when you start Windows, if you have an appropriate video card and enough computer memory to run Aero. If it is not on, to turn on the Aero feature, right-click the desktop, left-click Personalize, then select one of the Aero Themes.

Getting Started with Windows 7 — Windows 13

Clues to Use boxes provide
useful information related
to the lesson skill.

Tables provide helpful
summaries of key terms, buttons,
or keyboard shortcuts.

Assignments

The lessons in this book use Quest Specialty Travel, a fictional adventure travel company, as the case study. The assignments on the yellow pages at the end of each unit increase in difficulty. Case studies provide a variety of interesting and relevant business applications. Assignments include:

- **Concepts Reviews** consist of multiple choice, matching, and screen identification questions.
- **Skills Reviews** provide additional hands-on, step-by-step reinforcement.
- **Independent Challenges** are case projects requiring critical thinking and application of the unit skills. The Independent Challenges increase in difficulty, with the first one in each unit being the easiest. Independent Challenges 2 and 3 become increasingly open-ended, requiring more Independent problem solving.
- **Real Life Independent Challenges** are practical exercises in which students perform activities to help them with their every day lives.
- **Advanced Challenge Exercises** set within Independent Challenges provide optional steps for more advanced students.
- **Visual Workshops** are practical, self-graded capstone projects that require independent problem solving.

Instructor Resources

The Instructor Resources CD is Course Technology's way of putting the resources and information needed to teach and learn effectively into your hands. With an integrated array of teaching and learning tools that offer you and your students a broad range of technology-based instructional options, we believe this CD represents the highest quality and most cutting edge resources available to instructors today. Many of these resources are available at *www.cengage.com/coursetechnology*. The resources available with this book are:

- **Instructor's Manual**—Available as an electronic file, the Instructor's Manual includes detailed lecture topics with teaching tips for each unit.

- **Sample Syllabus**—Prepare and customize your course easily using this sample course outline.

- **PowerPoint Presentations**—Each unit has a corresponding PowerPoint presentation that you can use in lectures, distribute to your students, or customize to suit your course.

- **Figure Files**—The figures in the text are provided on the Instructor Resources CD to help you illustrate key topics or concepts. You can create traditional overhead transparencies by printing the figure files. Or you can create electronic slide shows by using the figures in a presentation program such as PowerPoint.

- **Solutions to Exercises**—Solutions to Exercises contains every file students are asked to create or modify in the lessons and end-of-unit material. Also provided in this section, there is a document outlining the solutions for the end-of-unit Concepts Review, Skills Review, and Independent Challenges. An Annotated Solution File and Grading Rubric accompany each file and can be used together for quick and easy grading.

- **ExamView**—ExamView is a powerful testing software package that allows you to create and administer printed, computer (LAN-based), and Internet exams. ExamView includes hundreds of questions that correspond to the topics covered in this text, enabling students to generate detailed study guides that include page references for further review. The computer-based and Internet testing components allow students to take exams at their computers, and also saves you time by grading each exam automatically.

COURSECASTS   **Learning on the Go. Always Available...Always Relevant.**

Our fast-paced world is driven by technology. You know because you are an active participant—always on the go, always keeping up with technological trends, and always learning new ways to embrace technology to power your life. Let CourseCasts, hosted by Ken Baldauf of Florida State University, be your guide to weekly updates in this ever-changing space. These timely, relevant podcasts are produced weekly and are available for download at http://coursecasts.course.com or directly from iTunes (search by CourseCasts). CourseCasts are a perfect solution to getting students (and even instructors) to learn on the go!

Read This Before You Begin

What do I need to use this book?

Computer: You need a computer that runs the Windows 7 operating system. The screens in this book show the Windows 7 Home Premium, but you can use this book if you have Windows 7 Ultimate or Windows 7 Professional.

Storage device: In Unit B, you save your files to a USB Flash drive. A USB Flash drive is a small, portable device that is sometimes called a thumbnail drive, a USB drive, a flash drive, or a keychain drive.

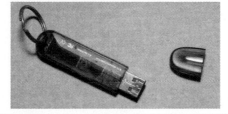

What if I don't have a USB Flash drive?

If you don't have a USB Flash drive, you can save your Unit B files and folders to a location on your hard disk drive (C:), such as your My Documents folder or a network drive. If you are using this book as part of a course, your instructor can tell you the best location to store your files.

Do I need Data Files to use this book?

No, you do not need any Data Files to use this book.

Do I need to be connected to the Internet to complete the steps and exercises in this book?

You do not need an Internet connection to complete the steps of Units A or B. However, in the Unit A end-of-unit exercises, Independent Challenge 3 does require an Internet connection.

What if my screen looks different from the figures shown in this book?

Resolution: This book was written and tested on computers with monitors set at a resolution of 1024 × 768. If your screen shows more or less information than the figures in this book, your monitor is probably set at a higher or lower resolution. If you don't see something on your screen, you might have to scroll down or up to see the object identified in the figure.

Window Size: As you use the Paint and WordPad accessory programs in these units, the command buttons in the Ribbon might appear differently, depending on the size of your program window. If your window is small, certain commands might be collapsed under one button, or the button name might be hidden. If you are unsure about a button's location, hold the mouse pointer over a button or click a list arrow and use the small boxes that appear to help you identify each item.

Transparent Windows: The screens shown in this book have transparent "glass" backgrounds and three dimensional effects, a set of special effects called **Windows Aero**. Aero is turned on automatically when you start Windows if you have an appropriate video card and enough computer memory to run Aero. If your computer does not show these effects, Aero might not be turned on. But this will not affect your work in these units. To turn Windows Aero on or off, right-click the Windows desktop, then left-click Personalize on the shortcut menu. In the Personalization options, click one of the Aero Themes. This book uses the Windows 7 Aero theme. To turn Aero off, select one of the Basic and High Contrast themes.

Author Acknowledgements

I sincerely thank Executive Editor Marjorie Hunt for giving me this opportunity and Senior Product Manager Christina Kling-Garrett for her expert guidance. Special thanks to Rachel Biheller Bunin for her amazing developmental editing and her many creative ideas. And I'm grateful to Bill for his endless patience and good humor and to Katharine, always, for her sage advice.

Getting Started with Windows 7

The Windows 7 operating system lets you use your computer. Windows 7 shares many features with other Windows programs, so once you learn how to work with Windows 7, you will find it easier to use the programs that run on your computer. In this unit, you learn to start Windows 7 and work with windows and other screen objects. You work with icons that represent programs and files, and you move and resize windows. As you use your computer, you will often have more than one window on your screen, so it's important that you learn how to manage them. As you complete this unit, you create a simple drawing in a program called Paint to help you learn how to use buttons, menus, and dialog boxes. After finding assistance in the Windows 7 Help and Support system, you end your Windows 7 session.  As a new Oceania tour manager for Quest Specialty Travel (QST), you need to develop basic Windows skills to keep track of tour bookings.

OBJECTIVES

Start Windows 7

Learn the Windows 7 desktop

Point and click

Start a Windows 7 program

Work with windows

Work with multiple windows

Use command buttons, menus, and dialog boxes

Get help

Exit Windows 7

Starting Windows 7

Windows 7 is an **operating system**, which is a program that lets you run your computer. A **program** is a set of instructions written for a computer. When you turn on your computer, the Windows 7 operating system starts automatically. If your computer did not have an operating system, you wouldn't see anything on the screen when you turn it on. For each user, the operating system can reserve a special area called a **user account** where each user can keep his or her own files. If your computer is set up for more than one user, you might need to **log in**, or select your user account name when the computer starts. If you are the only user on your computer, you won't have to select an account. You might also need to enter a **password**, a special sequence of numbers and letters each user can create. A password allows you to enter and use the files in your user account area. Users cannot see each others' account areas without their passwords, so passwords help keep your computer information secure. After you log in, you see a welcome message, and then the Windows 7 desktop. You will learn about the desktop in the next lesson. Your supervisor, Evelyn Swazey, asks you to start learning about the Windows 7 operating system.

1. **Push your computer's power button, which might look like or , then if the monitor is not turned on, press its power button to turn it on**

   On a desktop computer, the power button is probably on the front panel. On a laptop computer it's most likely at the top of the keys on your keyboard. After a few moments, a Starting Windows message appears. Then you might see a screen that lets you choose a user account, as shown in Figure A-1.

   > **TROUBLE**
   > If you do not see a screen that lets you choose a user account, go to Step 3.

2. **Click a user name if necessary**

   The name you click represents your user account that lets you use the computer. The user account may have your name assigned to it, or it might have a general name, like Student, or Lab User. A password screen may appear. If necessary, ask your instructor or technical support person which user account and password you should use.

   > **TROUBLE**
   > If you clicked the wrong user in Step 2, change to the correct user by clicking the Switch user button on the password screen.

3. **Type your password if necessary, using uppercase and lowercase letters as necessary, as shown in Figure A-2**

   Passwords are **case sensitive**, which means that if you type any letter using capital letters when lowercase letters are needed, Windows will not allow you to access your account. For example, if your password is "book", typing "Book" or "BOOK" will not let you enter your account. As you type your password, its characters appear as a series of dots on the screen. This makes it more difficult for anyone watching you to see your password, giving you additional security.

   > **TROUBLE**
   > If you type your password incorrectly, you see "The user name or password is incorrect." Click OK to try again. To help you remember, Windows shows the Password Hint that you entered when you created your password.

4. **Click the Go button**

   You see a welcome message, and then the Windows 7 desktop, shown in Figure A-3.

Getting Started with Windows 7

FIGURE A-1: Selecting a user name

Name and
picture
represent
each user's
account on
this computer

You might have
a different
version of
Windows 7

Ease of access
button shows
accessibility
options

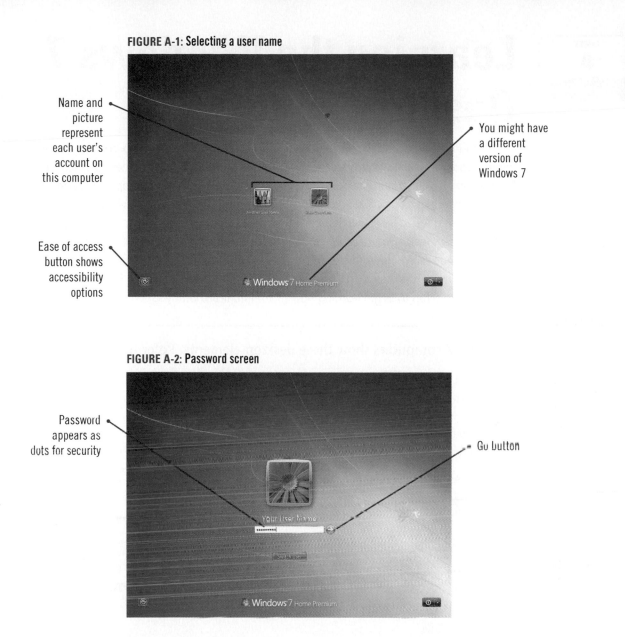

FIGURE A-2: Password screen

Password
appears as
dots for security

Go button

FIGURE A-3: Windows 7 desktop

Getting Started with Windows 7

Learning the Windows 7 Desktop

After Windows 7 starts up, you see the Windows 7 desktop. The **desktop** consists of a shaded or picture background with small graphics called icons. **Icons** are small images that represent items such as the Recycle Bin on your computer. You can rearrange, add, and delete desktop icons. Like an actual desktop, the Windows 7 desktop acts as your work area. You can use the desktop to manage the files and folders on your computer. A **file** is a collection of stored information, such as a letter, video, or program. A **folder** is a container that helps you organize your files, just like a cardboard folder on your desk. If you're using a new installation of Windows, the desktop might show only a Recycle Bin icon in the upper-left corner and the **taskbar**, the horizontal bar at the bottom of your screen. Evelyn asks you to explore the Windows 7 desktop to begin learning how to communicate with your computer.

DETAILS

Windows 7 computers show these desktop elements. Refer to Figure A-4.

*   **Start button**

    The **Start button** is your launching point when you want to communicate with your computer. You can use the Start button to start programs, to open windows that show you the contents of your computer, and to end your Windows session and turn off your computer.

QUICK TIP
If your taskbar is a different color than the one in Figure A-4, your computer might have different settings. This won't affect your work in this chapter.

*   **Taskbar**

    The **taskbar** is the horizontal bar at the bottom of the desktop. The taskbar contains the Start button as well as other buttons representing programs, folders, and files. You can use these buttons to immediately open programs or view files and programs that are on your computer.

*   **Notification area**

    The **notification area** at the right side of the taskbar contains icons that represent informational messages and programs you might find useful. It also contains information about the current date and time. Some programs automatically place icons here so they are easily available to you. The notification area also displays pop-up messages when something on your computer needs your attention.

*   **Recycle Bin**

    Like the wastepaper basket in your office, the **Recycle Bin** is where you place the files and folders that you don't need anymore and want to delete. All objects you place in the Recycle Bin stay there until you empty it. If you put an object there by mistake, you can easily retrieve it, as long as you haven't emptied the bin.

*   **Desktop background**

    The **desktop background** is the shaded area behind your desktop objects. You can change the desktop background to show different colors or even pictures.

You might see the following on your desktop:

*   **Icons and shortcuts**

    On the desktop background, you can place icons called **shortcuts**, which you can double-click to access programs, files, folders, and devices that you use frequently. That way, they are immediately available to you.

*   **Gadgets**

    Gadgets are optional programs that present helpful or entertaining information on your desktop. They include items such as clocks, current news headlines, calendars, picture albums, and weather reports. Some gadgets come with Windows 7 and you can easily place them on your desktop. You can download additional gadgets from the Internet. Figure A-5 shows a desktop that has a desktop background picture and shortcuts to programs, folders, and devices, as well as four gadgets.

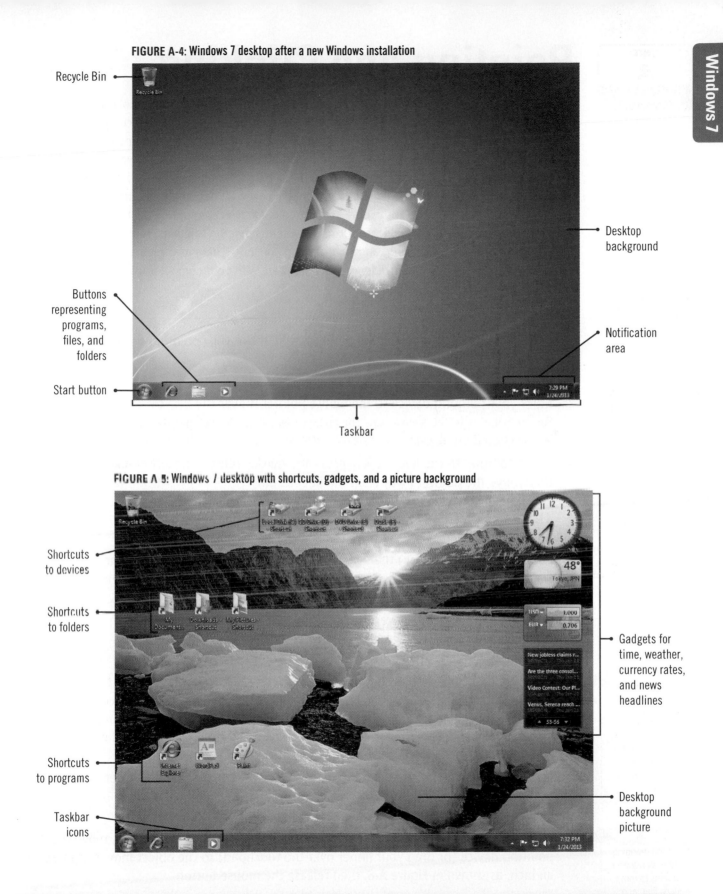

FIGURE A-4: Windows 7 desktop after a new Windows installation

Recycle Bin

Desktop background

Buttons representing programs, files, and folders

Notification area

Start button

Taskbar

FIGURE A-5: Windows 7 desktop with shortcuts, gadgets, and a picture background

Shortcuts to devices

Shortcuts to folders

Gadgets for time, weather, currency rates, and news headlines

Shortcuts to programs

Taskbar icons

Desktop background picture

What if my desktop looks different from these figures?

If you are using a computer that has been used by others, a different version of Windows 7, or a computer in a school lab, your desktop might be a different color, it might have a different design on it, or it might have different shortcuts and gadgets. Your Recycle Bin might be in a different desktop location. Don't be concerned with these differences. They will not interfere with your work in these units.

Pointing and Clicking

After you start Windows 7 and see the desktop, you can communicate with Windows using a pointing device. A **pointing device** controls the movement of the mouse pointer on your computer screen. The **mouse pointer** is a small arrow or other symbol that moves on the screen. The mouse pointer's shape changes depending on where you point and on the options available to you when you point. Your pointing device could be a mouse, trackball, touchpad, pointing stick, on-screen touch pointer, or a tablet. Figure A-6 shows some common pointing devices. A pointing device might be attached to your computer with a wire, connect wirelessly using an electronic signal, or it might be built into your computer. There are five basic **pointing device actions** you use to communicate with your computer: pointing, clicking, double-clicking, dragging, and right-clicking. Table A-1 describes each action. As you prepare to work on your tour schedule, you communicate with your computer using the basic pointing device actions.

STEPS

1. **Locate the mouse pointer on the desktop, then move your pointing device left, right, up, and down**

   The mouse pointer moves in the same direction as your pointing device.

2. **Move your pointing device so the mouse pointer is over the Recycle Bin**

   You are pointing to the Recycle Bin. The pointer shape is the **Select pointer** ▷ . The Recycle Bin icon becomes **highlighted,** looking as though it is framed in a box with a lighter color background and a border.

   QUICK TIP
   Use the tip of the pointer when pointing to an object.

3. **While pointing to the Recycle Bin, press and quickly release the left mouse button once, then move the pointer away from the Recycle Bin**

   Click a desktop icon once to **select** it, and then the interior of the border around it changes color. When you select an icon, you signal Windows 7 that you want to perform an action. You can also use pointing to identify screen items.

4. **Point to (but do not click) the Internet Explorer button** 🅔 **on the taskbar**

   The button border appears and an informational message called a **ScreenTip** identifies the program the button represents.

5. **Move the mouse pointer over the time and date in the notification area in the lower-right corner of the screen, read the ScreenTip, then click once**

   A pop-up window appears, containing a calendar and a clock displaying the current date and time.

   TROUBLE
   You need to double-click quickly, with a fast click-click, without moving the mouse. If a window didn't open, try again with a faster click-click.

6. **Place the tip of the mouse pointer over the Recycle Bin, then quickly click twice**

   You **double-clicked** the Recycle Bin. A window opens, showing the contents of the Recycle Bin, shown in Figure A-7. The area near the top of the screen is the **Address bar**, which shows the name of the item you have opened. If your Recycle Bin contains any discarded items, they appear in the white area below the Address bar. You can use single clicking to close a window.

7. **Place the tip of the mouse pointer over the Close button** ▬✕▬ **in the upper-right corner of the Recycle Bin window, notice the Close ScreenTip, then click once**

   The Recycle Bin window closes. You can use dragging to move icons on the desktop.

   QUICK TIP
   You'll use dragging in other Windows 7 programs to move folders, files, and other objects to new locations.

8. **Point to the Recycle Bin icon, press and hold down the left mouse button, move the pointing device (or drag your finger over the touchpad) so the object moves right about an inch, as shown in Figure A-8, then release the mouse button**

   You dragged the Recycle Bin icon to a new location.

9. **Repeat Step 8 to drag the Recycle Bin back to its original location**

FIGURE A-6: Pointing devices

Mouse

Trackball

Touchpad

Pointing stick

FIGURE A-7: Recycle Bin window

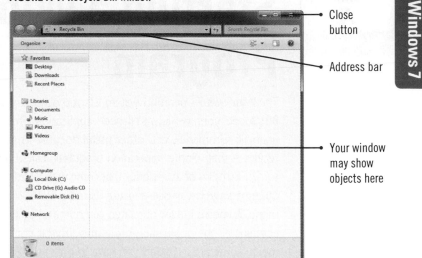

Close button

Address bar

Your window may show objects here

FIGURE A-8: Dragging the Recycle Bin icon

Releasing mouse button moves object to this location

TABLE A-1: Five pointing device actions

action	how to	use for
Pointing	Move the pointing device to position the tip of the pointer over an object, option, or item	Highlighting objects or options, or displaying informational boxes called ScreenTips
Clicking	Quickly press and release the left mouse button once	Selecting objects or commands, opening menus or items on the taskbar
Double-clicking	Quickly press and release the left mouse button twice	Opening programs, folders, or files represented by desktop icons
Dragging	Point to an object, press and hold down the left mouse button, move the object to a new location, then release the mouse button	Moving objects, such as icons on the desktop
Right-clicking	Point to an object, then press and release the right mouse button	Displaying a shortcut menu containing options specific to the object

Using right-clicking

For some actions, you click items using the right mouse button, known as right-clicking. You can **right-click** almost any icon on your desktop to open a shortcut menu. A **shortcut menu** lists common commands for an object. A **command** is an instruction to perform a task, such as emptying the Recycle Bin. The shortcut menu commands depend on the object you right-click. Figure A-9 shows the shortcut menu that appears if you right-click the Recycle Bin. Then you click (with the left mouse button) a shortcut menu command to issue that command.

FIGURE A-9: Right-click to show shortcut menu

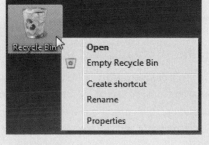

Open
Empty Recycle Bin

Create shortcut
Rename

Properties

Starting a Windows 7 Program

The Windows 7 operating system lets you operate your computer and see the programs and files it contains. But to do your work, you'll need application programs. **Application programs** let you create letters, financial summaries, and other useful documents as well as view Web pages on the Internet and send and receive e-mail. Some application programs, called **accessories**, come with Windows 7. (See Table A-2 for some examples of accessories that come with Windows 7.) To use an application program, you must start (or open) it so you can see and use its tools. With Windows 7 you start application programs using the Start menu. A **menu** is a list of related commands. You use the Start menu to open the All Programs menu, which contains all the application programs on your computer. You can see some programs on the All Programs menu; some are in folders you have to click first. To start a program, you click its name on the All Programs menu. ▓▓▓ Evelyn asks you to explore the Paint accessory program for creating brochure graphics.

STEPS

1. **Click the Start button ⊙ on the taskbar in the lower-left corner of screen**

   The Start menu opens, showing frequently used programs on the left side. The gray area on the right contains links to folders and other locations you are likely to use frequently. It also lets you get help and shut down your computer. See Figure A-10. Not all the programs available on your computer are shown.

2. **Point to All Programs**

   This menu shows programs installed on your computer. Your program list will differ, depending on what you (or your lab) have installed on your machine. Some program names are immediately available, and others are inside folders.

3. **Click the Accessories folder**

   A list of Windows accessory programs appears, as shown in Figure A-11. The program names are indented to the right from the Accessories folder, meaning that they are inside that folder.

4. **Move the 🖑 pointer over Paint and click once**

   The Paint program window opens on your screen, as shown in Figure A-12. When Windows opens an application program, it starts the program from your computer's hard disk, where it's permanently stored. Then it places the program in your computer's memory so you can use it.

5. **If your Paint window fills the screen completely, click the Restore Down button 🗗 in the upper-right corner of the window**

   If your Paint window doesn't look like Figure A-12, point to the lower-right corner of the window until the pointer becomes ⬉, then drag until it matches the figure.

Searching for programs and files using the Start menu

If you need to find a program, folder, or file on your computer quickly, the Search programs and files box on the Start menu can help. Click the Start button, then type the name of the item you want to find in the Search programs and files box. As you type, Windows 7 lists all programs, documents, e-mail messages, and files that contain the text you typed in a box above the Search box. The items appear as links, which means you only have to click the hand pointer 🖑 on the item you want, and Windows 7 opens it.

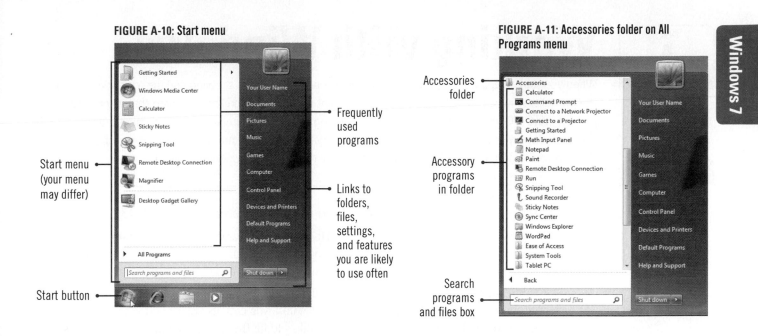

FIGURE A-10: Start menu

Start menu (your menu may differ)

Start button

Getting Started
Windows Media Center
Calculator
Sticky Notes
Snipping Tool
Remote Desktop Connection
Magnifier
Desktop Gadget Gallery

All Programs

Search programs and files

Your User Name
Documents
Pictures
Music
Games
Computer
Control Panel
Devices and Printers
Default Programs
Help and Support

Shut down

Frequently used programs

Links to folders, files, settings, and features you are likely to use often

FIGURE A-11: Accessories folder on All Programs menu

Accessories folder

Accessory programs in folder

Search programs and files box

Accessories
Calculator
Command Prompt
Connect to a Network Projector
Connect to a Projector
Getting Started
Math Input Panel
Notepad
Paint
Remote Desktop Connection
Run
Snipping Tool
Sound Recorder
Sticky Notes
Sync Center
Windows Explorer
WordPad
Ease of Access
System Tools
Tablet PC

Back

Search programs and files

Your User Name
Documents
Pictures
Music
Games
Computer
Control Panel
Devices and Printers
Default Programs
Help and Support

Shut down

FIGURE A-12: Paint program window

TABLE A-2: Some Windows 7 Accessory programs

accessory program name	use to
Math Input Panel	Interpret math expressions handwritten on a tablet and create a formula suitable for printing or inserting in another program
Notepad	Create text files with basic text formatting
Paint	Create and edit drawings using lines, shapes, and colors
Snipping Tool	Capture an image of any screen area that you can save to use in a document
Sticky Notes	Create short text notes that you can use to set reminders or create to-do lists for yourself
Windows Explorer	View and organize the files and folders on your computer
WordPad	Type letters or other text documents with formatting

Working with Windows

When you start an application program, its **program window** opens, showing you the tools you need to use the program. A new, blank file also opens. In the Paint program, you create a drawing that you can save as a file and print. All windows in the Windows 7 operating system have similar window elements. Once you can use a window in one program, you can then work with windows in many other programs. As you develop your tour marketing plans, you work with the open Paint window using Windows 7 elements.

DETAILS

Many windows have the following common elements. Refer to Figure A-13:

- At the top of every open window, you see a **title bar**, a transparent or solid-colored strip that contains the name of the program and document you opened. This document has not been saved, so it has the temporary name "Untitled." On the right side of the title bar, you see three icons.

  The **Minimize button** temporarily hides the window, making it a button on the taskbar. The program is still running, but its window is hidden until you click its taskbar button to display it again. The **Maximize button** enlarges the window to fill the entire computer screen. If a window is already maximized, the Maximize button changes to the **Restore Down button**. Restoring a window reduces it to the last nonmaximized size. The **Close button** closes the program. To use it later, you need to start it again.

- Many windows have a **scroll bar** on the right side and/or on the bottom of the window. You click the scroll bar elements to show parts of your document that are hidden below the bottom edge or off to the right side of the screen. See Table A-3 to learn the parts of a scroll bar.

- Just below the title bar, at the top of the Paint window, is the **Ribbon**, a strip that contains tabs. **Tabs** are pages that contain buttons that you click to perform actions. The Paint window has two tabs, the Home tab and the View tab. Tabs are divided into **groups** of command buttons. The Home tab has five groups: Clipboard, Image, Tools, Shapes, and Colors. Some programs have **menus**, words you click to show lists of commands, and **toolbars**, containing program buttons.

- The **Quick Access toolbar**, in the upper-left corner of the window, lets you quickly perform common actions such as saving a file.

> **QUICK TIP**
> If your Ribbon looks different from Figure A-13, your window is a little narrower. A narrow window collapses some buttons so you can only see group names. In that case, you might need to click a group name to see buttons.

STEPS

1. **Click the Paint window Minimize button**
   The program is now represented only by its button on the taskbar. See Figure A-14. The taskbar button for the Paint program now has a gradient background with blue and white shading. Taskbar buttons for closed programs have a solid blue background.

2. **Click the taskbar button representing the Paint program**
   The program window reappears.

3. **Drag the Paint scroll box down, notice the lower edge of the Paint canvas that appears, then click the Paint Up scroll arrow until you see the top edge of the canvas**
   In the Ribbon, the Home tab is in front of the View tab.

4. **Point to the View tab with the tip of the mouse pointer, then click the View tab once**
   The View tab moves in front of the Home tab and shows commands for viewing your drawings. The View tab has three groups: Zoom, Show or hide, and Display.

5. **Click the Home tab**

6. **Click the Paint window Maximize button**
   The window fills the screen and the Maximize button becomes the Restore Down button.

7. **Click the Paint window's Restore Down button**
   The Paint window returns to its previous size on the screen.

> **TROUBLE**
> If your screen resolution is set higher than 1024 × 768, you might not see a scroll box. You can continue with the lesson.

> **QUICK TIP**
> To quickly restore down the selected window, press and hold down the key and then press the down arrow key.

FIGURE A-13: Paint program window elements

Quick Access toolbar

Paint program button

Ribbon

Tabs

Window control buttons

Title bar

Scroll bar

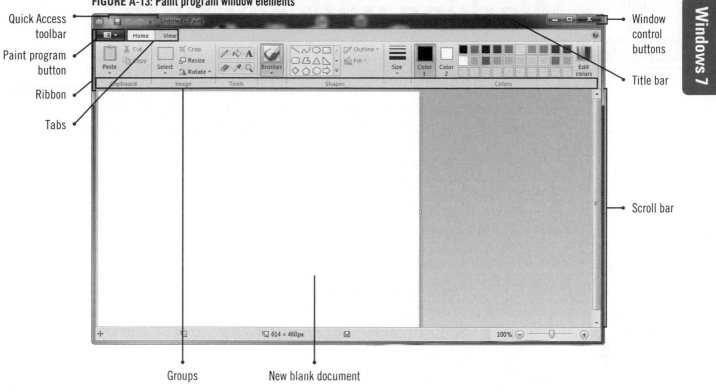

Groups

New blank document

FIGURE A-14: Taskbar showing Paint program button

Paint program button with gradient background indicates program is open

TABLE A-3: Parts of a scroll bar

name	looks like	use for
Scroll box	▤ (Size may vary)	Drag to scroll quickly through a long document
Scroll arrows	▲ ▼	Click to scroll up or down in small amounts
Shaded area	(Above and below scroll box)	Click to move up or down by one screen

Using the Quick Access toolbar

On the left side of the title bar, the Quick Access toolbar lets you perform common tasks with just one click. The Save button 🖫 saves the changes you have made to a document. The Undo button 🖘 lets you reverse (undo) the last action you performed. The Redo button 🖙 reinstates the change you just undid. Use the Customize Quick Access Toolbar button ▾ to add other frequently used buttons to the toolbar, move the toolbar below the Ribbon, or hide the Ribbon.

Working with Multiple Windows

Windows 7 lets you work with more than one program at a time. If you open two or more programs, a window opens for each one. You can work with each open program window, going back and forth between them. The window in front is called the **active window**. Any other open window behind the active window is called an **inactive window**. For ease in working with multiple windows, you can move, arrange, make them smaller or larger, minimize, or restore them so they're not in the way. To resize a window, drag a window's edge, called its **border**. You can also use the taskbar to switch between windows. See Table A-4 for a summary of taskbar actions. Keeping the Paint program open, you open the WordPad program and work with the Paint and WordPad program windows.

STEPS

1. **With the Paint window open, click the Start button ⊕, point to All Programs, click the Accessories folder, then click WordPad**

   The WordPad window opens in front of the Paint window. See Figure A-15. The WordPad window is in front, indicating that it is the active window. The Paint window is the inactive window. On the taskbar, the gradient backgrounds on the WordPad and Paint program buttons on the taskbar tell you that both programs are open. You want to move the WordPad window out of the way so you can see both windows at once.

   > **QUICK TIP**
   > To click an inactive window to make it active, click its title bar, window edge, or a blank area. To move a window, you must drag its title bar.

2. **Point to a blank part of the WordPad window title bar, then drag the WordPad window so you can see more of the Paint window**

3. **Click once on the Paint window's title bar**

   The Paint window is now the active window and appears in front of the WordPad window. You can make any window active by clicking it. You can use the taskbar to do the same thing. You can also move among open program windows by pressing and holding down the [Alt] key on your keyboard and pressing the [Tab] key. A small window opens in the middle of the screen, showing miniature versions of each open program window. Each time you press [Tab], you select the next open program window. When you release [Tab] and [Alt], the selected program window becomes active.

   > **QUICK TIP**
   > To instantly minimize all inactive windows, point to the active window's title bar, and quickly "shake" the window back and forth. This feature is called Aero Shake.

4. **On the taskbar, click the WordPad window button 🖼**

   The WordPad window is now active. When you open multiple windows on the desktop, you may need to resize windows so they don't get in the way of other open windows. You can use dragging to resize a window.

   > **TROUBLE**
   > Point to any edge of a window until you see the ⟷ or ↕ pointer and drag to make it larger or smaller in one direction only.

5. **Point to the lower-right corner of the WordPad window until the pointer becomes ⬦, then drag up and to the left about an inch to make the window smaller**

   Windows 7 has a special feature that lets you automatically resize a window so it fills half the screen.

6. **Point to the WordPad window title bar, drag the window to the left side of the screen until the mouse pointer reaches the screen edge and the left half of the screen turns a transparent blue color, then release the mouse button**

   The WordPad window "snaps" to fill the left side of the screen.

7. **Point to the Paint window title bar, then drag the window to the right side of the screen until it snaps to fill the right half of the screen**

   The Paint window fills the right side of the screen. The Snap feature makes it easy to arrange windows side by side to view the contents of both at the same time.

8. **Click the WordPad window Close button ❌ then click the Maximize button ◻ in the Paint window's title bar**

   The WordPad program closes, so you can no longer use its tools unless you open it again. The Paint program window remains open and fills the screen.

FIGURE A-15: WordPad window in front of Paint window

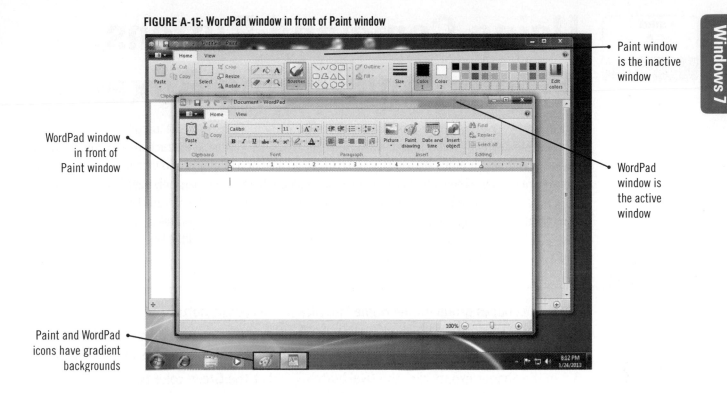

Paint window is the inactive window

WordPad window in front of Paint window

WordPad window is the active window

Paint and WordPad icons have gradient backgrounds

TABLE A-4: Using the Windows taskbar

to	do this
Add buttons to taskbar	Drag a program name from the Start menu over the taskbar, until a ScreenTip reads Pin to Taskbar
Change order of taskbar buttons	Drag any icon to a new taskbar location
See a list of recent documents opened in a taskbar program	Right-click taskbar program button
Close a document using the taskbar	Point to taskbar button, point to document name in jump list, then click Close button
Minimize all open windows	Click Show desktop button to the right of taskbar date and time
Redisplay all minimized windows	Click Show desktop button to the right of taskbar date and time
Make all windows transparent (Aero only)	Point to Show desktop button to the right of taskbar date and time
See preview of documents in taskbar (Aero only)	Point to taskbar button for open program

Switching windows with Windows Aero

Windows Aero is a set of special effects for Windows 7. If your windows have transparent "glass" backgrounds like those shown in the figures in this book, your Aero feature is turned on. Your windows show subtle animations when you minimize, maximize, and move windows. When you arrange windows using Aero, your windows can appear in a three-dimensional stack that you can quickly view without having to click the taskbar. To achieve this effect, called **Aero Flip 3D**, press and hold [Ctrl][⊞], then press [Tab]. Press [Tab] repeatedly to move through the stack, then press [Enter] to enlarge the document in the front of the stack. In addition, when you point to a taskbar button, Aero shows you small previews of the document, photo, or video—a feature called **Aero Peek**. Aero is turned on automatically when you start Windows, if you have an appropriate video card and enough computer memory to run Aero. If it is not on, to turn on the Aero feature, right-click the desktop, left-click Personalize, then select one of the Aero Themes.

Using Command Buttons, Menus, and Dialog Boxes

When you work in an open program window, you communicate with the program using command buttons, menus, and dialog boxes. **Command buttons** let you issue instructions to modify program objects. Command buttons are sometimes organized on a Ribbon into tabs, and then into groups like those in the Paint window. Some command buttons have text on them, and others only have icons that represent what they do. Other command buttons reveal **menus**, lists of commands you can choose. And some command buttons open up a **dialog box**, a window with controls that lets you tell Windows what you want. Table A-5 lists the common types of controls you find in dialog boxes. You use command buttons, menus, and dialog boxes to communicate with the Paint program.

STEPS

QUICK TIP
If you need to move the oval, use the keyboard arrow keys to move it left, right, up, or down.

1. In the Shapes group on the Home tab, click the Rectangle button ☐
2. In the Colors group, click the Gold button ▨, move the pointer over the white drawing area, called the canvas, then drag to draw a rectangle a similar size to the one in Figure A-16
3. In the Shapes group, click the Oval button ⬭, click the Green color button ▨ in the Colors group, then drag a small oval above the rectangle, using Figure A-16 as a guide

TROUBLE
Don't be concerned if your object isn't exactly like the one in the figure.

4. Click the Fill with color icon in the Tools group, click the Light turquoise color button in the Colors group, click inside the oval, click the Purple color button, then click inside the rectangle, and compare your drawing to Figure A-16
5. In the Image group, click the Select list arrow, then click Select all, as shown in Figure A-17
    The Select menu has several menu commands. The Select all command selects the entire drawing, as indicated by the dotted line surrounding the white drawing area.
6. In the Image group, click the Rotate or flip button, then click Rotate right 90°
7. Click the Paint menu button ▮▾ just below the title bar, then click Print
    The Print dialog box opens, as shown in Figure A-18. This dialog box lets you choose a printer, specify which part of your document or drawing you want to print, and choose how many copies you want to print. The **default**, or automatically selected, number of copies is 1, which is what you want.

TROUBLE
If you prefer not to print your document, click Cancel.

8. Click Print
    The drawing prints on your printer. You decide to close the program without saving your drawing.
9. Click ▮▾ , click Exit, then click Don't Save

TABLE A-5: Common dialog box controls

element	example	description
Text box	132	A box in which you type text or numbers
Spin box	1 ▴▾	A box with up and down arrows; click arrows or type to increase or decrease value
Option button	○ ◉	A small circle you click to select the option
Check box	☑	Turns an option on when checked or off when unchecked
List box	Select Printer / Add Printer / Dell Laser Printer 3000cn PCL6 / Fax	A box that lets you select an option from a list of options
Command button	Save	A button that completes or cancels the selected settings

FIGURE A-16: Rectangle and oval shapes with fill

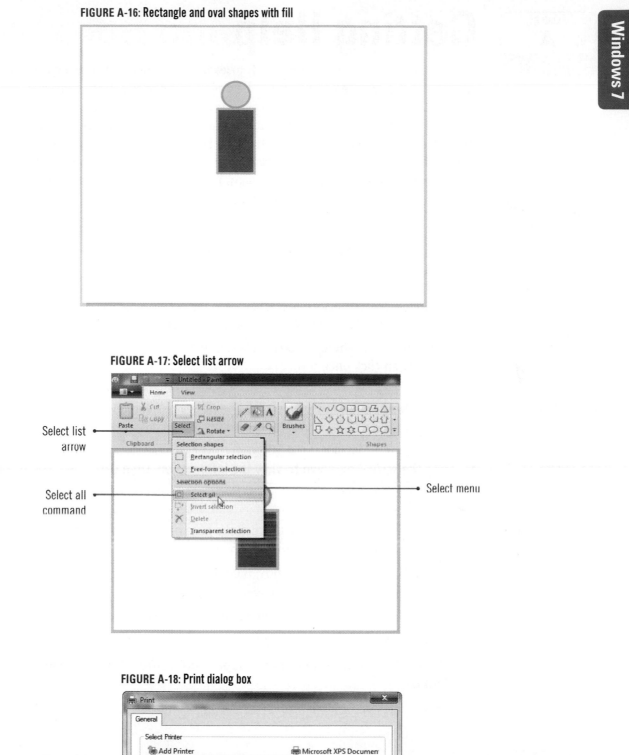

FIGURE A-17: Select list arrow

Select list arrow

Select all command

Select menu

FIGURE A-18: Print dialog box

Your printer name may differ

One cop is the default

Getting Help

As you use Windows 7, you might feel ready to learn more about it, or you might have a problem and need some advice. You can open the Windows 7 Help and Support to find information you need. You can browse Help and Support topics by clicking a category, such as "Learn about Windows Basics." Within this category, you see more specific categories. Each category has topics in blue or purple text called **links** that you can click to learn more. You can also search Help and Support by typing one or more descriptive words called **keywords**, such as "taskbar," to ask Windows to find topics related to your keywords. The Help toolbar contains icons that give you more Help options. Table A-6 describes the Help toolbar icons. You use Windows 7 help to learn more about Windows and the WordPad accessory.

STEPS

> **TROUBLE**
> If your computer is not connected to the Internet, you will see an alert at the top of the Help window. You can continue with the steps in this lesson.

1. **Click the Start button 🔵, then on the right side of the Start menu, click Help and Support**
   The Windows Help and Support window opens, as shown in Figure A-19. A search box appears near the top of the window. Three topics appear as blue or purple text, meaning that they are links. Below them, you see descriptive text and a link to a Web site that contains more information about Windows.

2. **Under Not sure where to start?, position the hand pointer 👆 over Learn about Windows Basics, then click once**
   Several categories of Windows Basics topics appear, with links under each one.

> **QUICK TIP**
> If you are using a mouse with a scroll wheel, you can use the scroll wheel to scroll up and down. If you are using a touchpad, the right side of your touchpad might let you scroll.

3. **Under Desktop fundamentals, click The desktop (overview)**
   Help and Support information about the desktop appears, divided into several categories. Some of the text appears as a blue or purple link.

4. **Drag the scroll box down to view the information, then drag the scroll box back to the top of the scroll bar**
   You decide to learn more about the taskbar.

5. **Under The desktop (overview), click the blue or purple text The taskbar (overview), then scroll down and read the information about the taskbar**

> **QUICK TIP**
> Search text is not case sensitive. Typing wordpad, Wordpad, or WordPad finds the same results.

6. **Click in the Search Help text box, type wordpad, then click the Search Help button 🔍**
   A list of links related to the WordPad accessory program appears. See Figure A-20.

7. **Click Using WordPad, scroll down if necessary, then click Create, open, and save documents**

8. **Scroll down and view the information, clicking any other links that interest you**

9. **Click the Close button ✖ in the upper-right corner of the Windows Help and Support window**
   The Windows Help and Support window closes.

TABLE A-6: Help toolbar icons

help toolbar icon	name	action
🔵	Help and Support home	Displays the Help and Support Home page
🖨	Print	Prints the currently-displayed help topic
📖	Browse Help	Displays a list of Help topics organized by subject
🔍 Ask	Ask	Describes other ways to get help
Options ▾	Options	Lets you print, browse, search, set Help text size, and adjust settings

FIGURE A-19: Windows Help and Support window

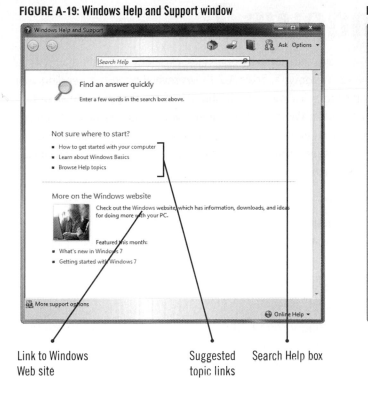

FIGURE A-20: Results of a search on WordPad

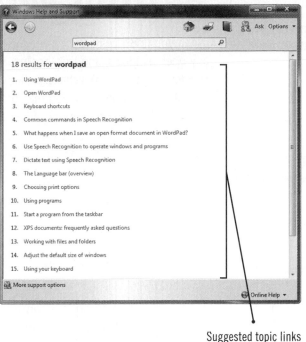

Link to Windows
Web site

Suggested
topic links

Search Help box

Suggested topic links
(your links may differ)

Finding other ways to get help

As you use Windows 7, you might want more help than you can find by clicking links or searching. You will find many other methods in the Windows Help and Support Home window. Click the Windows website link to locate blogs (Web logs, which are personal commentaries), downloads, Windows 7 video tours, and other current Windows 7 resources. Click the Ask button in the Help and Support window toolbar to learn about **Windows Remote Assistance**, which lets you connect with another computer, perhaps that of a trusted friend or instructor, so they can operate your computer using an Internet connection. The same window lets you open Microsoft Answers. **Microsoft Answers** is a website the lets you search **forums** (electronic gathering places where anyone can add questions and answers on computer issues), Microsoft help files, and even on-screen video demonstrations about selected topics.

Exiting Windows 7

When you finish working on your computer, save and close any open files, close any open programs, close any open windows, and exit (or **shut down**) Windows 7. Table A-7 shows several options for ending your Windows 7 sessions. Whichever option you choose, it's important to shut down your computer in an orderly way. If you turn off or unplug the computer while Windows 7 is running, you could lose data or damage Windows 7 and your computer. If you are working in a computer lab, follow your instructor's directions and your lab's policies for ending your Windows 7 session. ▧▧▧▧ You have examined the basic ways you can use Windows 7, so you are ready to end your Windows 7 session.

STEPS

1. **Click the Start button ⊕ on the taskbar**

   The lower-right corner of the Start menu lets you shut down your computer. It also displays a menu with other options for ending a Windows 7 session.

   TROUBLE
   If a previous user has customized your computer, your button and menu commands might be in different locations. For example, the Power button may show "Restart," and "Shut down" may appear on the menu.

2. **Point to the Power button list arrow ▣, as shown in Figure A-21**

   The Power button menu lists other shutdown options.

3. **If you are working in a computer lab, follow the instructions provided by your instructor or technical support person for ending your Windows 7 session. If you are working on your own computer, click Shut down or the option you prefer for ending your Windows 7 session**

4. **After you shut down your computer, you may also need to turn off your monitor and other hardware devices, such as a printer, to conserve energy**

Installing updates when you exit Windows

Sometimes, after you shut down your machine, you might find that your machine does not shut down immediately. Instead, Windows might install software updates. If your power button shows this yellow icon ▣, that means that Windows will install updates on your next shutdown. If you see a window indicating that updates are being installed, do not unplug or press the power switch to turn off your machine. Allow the updates to install completely. After the updates are installed, your computer will shut down, as you originally requested.

FIGURE A-21: Shutting down your computer

Power button

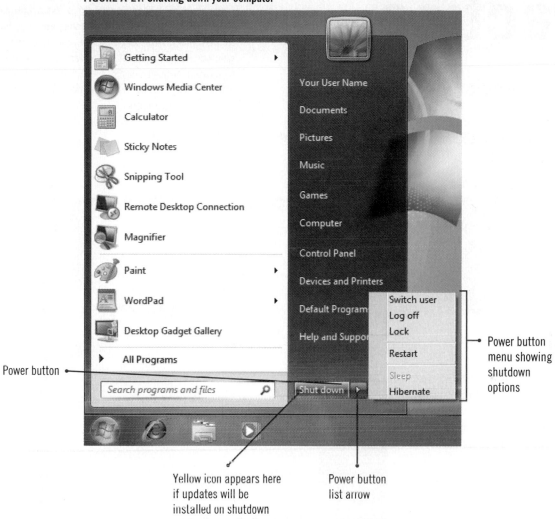

Power button
menu showing
shutdown
options

Yellow icon appears here
if updates will be
installed on shutdown

Power button
list arrow

TABLE A-7: Options for ending a Windows 7 session

option	description	click
Shut down	Completely turns off your computer	Start button, Shut down
Switch user	Locks your user account and displays the Welcome screen so another user can log on	Start button, Power button list arrow, Switch user
Log off	Closes all windows, programs, and documents, then displays the Log in screen	Start button, Power button list arrow, Log off
Lock	Locks computer so only current user (or administrator) can use it	Start button, Power button list arrow, Lock
Restart	Shuts down your computer, then restarts it	Start button, Power button list arrow, Restart
Sleep	Puts computer in a low-power state while preserving your session in the computer's memory	Start button, Power button list arrow, Sleep
Hibernate	Turns off computer drives and screens but saves image of your work; when you turn machine on, it starts where you left off	Start button, Power button list arrow, Hibernate

Practice

SAM

For current SAM information, including versions and content details, visit SAM Central (http://samcentral.course.com). If you have a SAM user profile, you may have access to hands-on instruction, practice, and assessment of the skills covered in this unit. Since various versions of SAM are supported throughout the life of this text, check with your instructor for the correct instructions and URL/Web site for accessing assignments.

Concepts Review

Label the elements of the Windows 7 window shown in Figure A-22.

FIGURE A-22

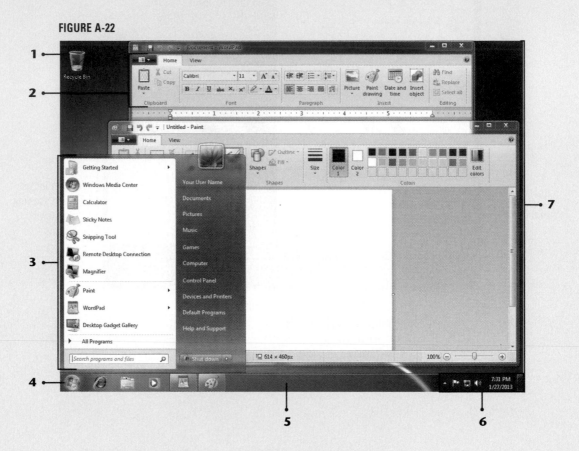

Match each term with the statement that best describes it.

8. **Accessory**
9. **Keyword**
10. **Trackball**
11. **Active window**
12. **Password**
13. **Operating system**
14. **Taskbar**

a. A sequence of numbers and letters users create to keep information secure
b. The window in front of other windows
c. Horizontal strip at bottom of screen that contains buttons
d. A pointing device
e. Application program that comes with Windows 7
f. Descriptive word you use to search Windows Help and Support
g. A program necessary to run your computer

Select the best answer from the list of choices.

15. **What part of a window shows the name of the program you opened?**
   a. Title bar
   b. Scroll bar
   c. Ribbon
   d. Quick Access toolbar

16. **You use the Maximize button to:**
   a. Restore a window to a previous size.
   b. Expand a window to fill the entire screen.
   c. Temporarily hide a window.
   d. Scroll down a window.

17. **Which of the following is not an accessory program?**
   a. Snipping Tool
   b. Paint
   c. WordPad
   d. Windows 7

18. **Which button do you click to reduce an open window to a button on the taskbar?**
   a. Maximize button
   b. Restore Down button
   c. Minimize button
   d. Close button

19. **Right-clicking is an action that:**
   a. Starts a program.
   b. Requires a password.
   c. Displays a shortcut menu.
   d. Opens the taskbar.

20. **The Windows 7 feature that shows windows with transparent "glass" backgrounds is:**
   a. Paint.
   b. Aero.
   c. Taskbar.
   d. Sticky Notes.

21. **Windows 7 is a(n):**
   a. Accessory program.
   b. Application program.
   c. Operating system.
   d. Gadget.

Skills Review

1. **Start Windows 7.**
   a. If your computer and monitor are not running, press your computer's and your monitor's power buttons.
   b. If necessary, click the user name that represents your user account.
   c. Enter a password if necessary, using correct uppercase and lowercase letters.

2. **Learn the Windows 7 desktop.**
   a. Examine the Windows 7 desktop to identify the Start button, the taskbar, the notification area, the Recycle Bin, the desktop background, desktop icons, and gadgets, if any.

3. **Point and click.**
   a. On the Windows desktop, select the Recycle Bin.
   b. Open the Start menu, then close it.
   c. Open the clock and calendar on the right side of the taskbar.
   d. Click the desktop to close the calendar.
   e. Open the Recycle Bin window, then close it.

4. **Start a Windows 7 program.**
   a. Use the Start button to open the Start menu.
   b. Open the All Programs menu.
   c. On the All Programs menu, open the Accessories folder.
   d. Open the WordPad accessory.

5. **Work with Windows.**
   a. Minimize the WordPad window.
   b. Redisplay it using a taskbar button.
   c. In the WordPad window, click the WordPad button in the Ribbon, then click the About WordPad command. (*Hint*: The WordPad button is next to the Home tab.)
   d. Close the About WordPad window.
   e. Maximize the WordPad window, then restore it down.
   f. Display the View tab in the WordPad window.

Skills Review (continued)

6. Work with multiple windows.

   a. Leaving WordPad open, open Paint.

   b. Make the WordPad window the active window.

   c. Make the Paint window the active window.

   d. Minimize the Paint window.

   e. Drag the WordPad window so it automatically fills the left side of the screen.

   f. Redisplay the Paint window.

   g. Drag the Paint window so it automatically fills the right side of the screen.

   h. Close the WordPad window, maximize the Paint window, then restore down the Paint window.

7. Use command buttons, menus, and dialog boxes.

FIGURE A-23

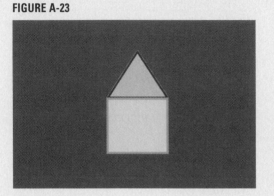

   a. In the Paint window, draw a red triangle, similar to Figure A-23.

   b. Use the Fill with color button to fill the triangle with a gold color.

   c. Draw a green rectangle just below the triangle.

   d. Use the Fill with color button to fill the green triangle with a light turquoise color.

   e. Fill the drawing background with purple and compare your drawing with Figure A-23.

   f. Use the Select list arrow and menu to select the entire drawing, then use the Rotate or flip command to rotate the drawing left 90°.

   g. Close the Paint program without saving the drawing.

8. Get help.

   a. Open the Windows Help and Support window.

   b. Open the "How to get started with your computer" topic.

   c. Open the "First week tasks" topic, click a link called "Create a user account", then read the topic information.

   d. In the Search Help text box, search for help about user accounts.

   e. Find the link that describes what a user account is and click it.

   f. Read the topic, then close the Windows Help and Support window.

9. Exit Windows 7.

   a. Shut down your computer using the Shut down command or the command for your work or school setting.

   b. Turn off your monitor.

Independent Challenge 1

You work for Will's Percussion, an Oregon manufacturer of drums and drumsticks. The company ships percussion instruments and supplies to music stores and musicians in the United States and Canada. The owner, Will, gives seminars at drummer conventions on how to avoid repetitive stress injuries to the hands and arms. He knows this can also be a big problem for computer users as well, so he asks you to research the topic and write some guidelines for the company's employees.

   a. Start your computer, log on to Windows 7 if necessary, then open Windows Help and Support.

   b. Click the Learn about Windows Basics link.

   c. In the Learn about your computer section, read the topic about using your mouse.

   d. At the bottom of the topic, read the Tips for using your mouse safely.

   e. Using pencil and paper, write a short memo to Will listing, in your own words, the most important tips for avoiding soreness or injury when using a mouse. Close the Windows Help and Support window, then exit Windows.

Independent Challenge 2

You are the new manager for Katharine Anne's Designs, a business that supplies floral arrangements to New York businesses. The company maintains four delivery vans that supply flowers to various locations. Katharine asks you to investigate how the Windows 7 Calculator accessory can help her company be a responsible energy consumer.

Independent Challenge 2 (continued)

a. Start your computer, log on to Windows 7 if necessary, then open the Windows 7 accessory called Calculator.

b. Drag the Calculator window to place it in the lower-left corner of the desktop just above the taskbar.

c. Minimize the Calculator window, then redisplay it.

d. Click to enter the number 87 on the Calculator.

e. Click the division sign (/) button.

f. Click the number 2.

g. Click the equals sign button (=), and write the result shown in the Calculator window on a piece of paper. See Figure A-24.

h. Click the Help menu in the Calculator window, then click View Help. In the Using Calculator window, determine the three ways of entering calculations in the Calculator. Write the three methods on your handwritten list.

i. Close the Help window.

FIGURE A-24

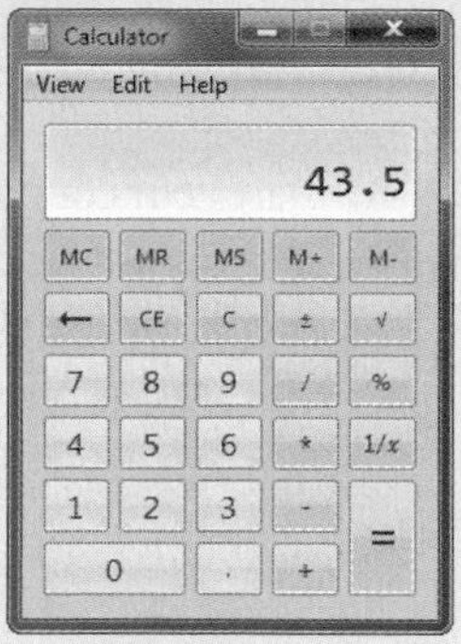

Advanced Challenge Exercise

- Open the View menu on the Calculator window, and click Date calculation.
- Click the list arrow under Select the date calculation you want, then click Calculate the difference between two dates.
- Write how Katharine's business might use this to calculate the length of time it takes a customer to pay an invoice.
- Click the View menu, point to Worksheets, then click Fuel economy (mpg).
- Click in the Distance (miles) text box and enter 100; click in the Fuel used (gallons) text box and type 5, then use the Calculate button to calculate the mileage.
- Write a short paragraph on how Katharine can use this feature to help calculate her van mileage.
- Click the View menu and return to the Basic view.
- Try to click the Calculator window's Maximize button. Note the result and add this fact to your document.

j. Close the Calculator, then exit Windows.

Independent Challenge 3

You are the office manager for Peter's Pet Shipping, a service business in Vancouver, BC that specializes in air shipping of cats and dogs to Canada and the northern United States. It's important to know the temperature in the destination city, so that the animals won't be in danger from extreme temperatures when they are unloaded from the aircraft. Peter has asked you to find a way to easily monitor temperatures in destination cities. You decide to use a Windows gadget so you can see current temperatures in Celsius on your desktop.

To complete this Independent Challenge, you need an Internet connection. You also need permission to add gadgets to the Windows Desktop. If you are working in a computer lab, check with your instructor or technical support person.

a. Start your computer, log on to Windows 7 if necessary, then click the Start button, open the All Programs menu, then click Desktop Gadget Gallery.

b. Double-click the Weather gadget, then close the Gallery window.

c. Move the pointer over the Weather gadget on the desktop, then notice the small buttons that appear on its right side.

d. Click the Larger size button (the middle button).

e. Click the Options button (the third button down) to open the weather options window.

f. In the Select current location text box, type Juneau, Alaska, then click the Search button.

g. Verify that the window shows the current location as "Juneau, Alaska."

h. Click the Celsius option button, then click OK.

i. To close the gadget, point to the gadget, then click the Close button (the top button).

j. Write Peter a memo outlining how you can use the Windows Weather gadget to help keep pets safe, then exit Windows.

Real Life Independent Challenge

As a professional photographer, you often evaluate pictures. You decide to explore a Windows Desktop gadget that will let you display a slide show on your desktop using photos you choose.

To complete this Independent Challenge, you need an Internet connection. You also need permission to add gadgets to the Windows Desktop. If you are working in a computer lab, check with your instructor or technical support person.

a. Start your computer, log on to Windows 7 if necessary, click the Start button, open the All Programs menu, then click Desktop Gadget Gallery.

b. Double-click the Slide Show gadget, then close the Gallery window.

c. Move the pointer over the Slide Show gadget on the desktop, then notice the small buttons that appear on its right side.

d. Click the Larger size button (the second button down).

e. Click the Options button (the third button down) to open the Slide Show options window.

f. Click the Folder list arrow and click the My Pictures folder. If you do not have pictures on your computer, click the Sample Pictures folder.

g. Click the Show each picture list arrow and select a duration.

h. Click the Transition between pictures list arrow and select a transition.

i. If you want the pictures to be in random order, click the Shuffle pictures check box.

j. Click OK.

Advanced Challenge Exercise

- Place the mouse pointer over the Slide Show window, then right-click.
- Point to Opacity and left-click an opacity level, then move the mouse pointer over the desktop. Adjust the opacity to the level you prefer.
- Drag the gadget to the desktop location you choose.

k. View your slide show, click the Slide Show window's Close button, then exit Windows.

Visual Workshop

As owner of Icons Plus, an icon design business, you decide to customize your desktop and resize your Help window to better suit your needs as you work with Paint. Organize your screen as shown in Figure A-25. Note the position of the Recycle Bin, the location of the Paint window, and the size and location of the Help and Support window. Write a paragraph summarizing how you used clicking and dragging to make your screen look like Figure A-25. Then exit Windows.

FIGURE A-25

Understanding File Management

To work with the folders and files on your computer, you need to understand how your computer stores them. You should also know how to organize them so you can always find the information you need. These skills are called **file management** skills. When you create a document and save it as a file, it is important that you save the file in a place where you can find it later. To keep your computer files organized, you will need to copy, move, and rename them. When you have files you don't need any more, it's a good idea to move or delete them so your computer has only current files.  Your supervisor, Evelyn Swazey, asks you to learn how to manage your computer files so you can begin creating and organizing documents for the upcoming Oceania tours.

OBJECTIVES

Understand folders and files

Create and save a file

Explore the files and folders on your computer

Change file and folder views

Open, edit, and save files

Copy files

Move and rename files

Search for files, folders, and programs

Delete and restore files

Understanding Folders and Files

As you work with your computer programs, you create and save files, such as letters, drawings, or budgets. When you save files, you usually save them inside folders, which are storage areas on your computer. You use folders to group related files, as with paper folders in a file cabinet. The files and folders on your computer are organized in a **file hierarchy**, a system that arranges files and folders in different levels, like the branches of a tree. Figure B-1 shows a sample file hierarchy. Evelyn asks you to look at some important facts about files and folders to help you store your Oceania tour files.

DETAILS

Use the following guidelines as you organize files using your computer's file hierarchy:

• **Use folders and subfolders to organize files**

As you work with your computer, you can add folders to your hierarchy and rename them to help you organize your work. You should give folders unique names that help you easily identify them. You can also create **subfolders**, which are folders that are inside of other folders. Windows comes with several existing folders, such as My Documents, My Music, and My Pictures, that you can use as a starting point.

• **View files in windows**

You view your computer contents by opening a **window**, like the one in Figure B-2. A window is divided into sections. The **Navigation pane** on the left side of the window shows the folder structure on your computer. When you click a folder in the Navigation pane, you see its contents in the **File list** on the right side. The **Details pane** at the bottom of the window provides information about selected files in the File list. A window actually opens in an accessory program called **Windows Explorer**, although the program name does not appear on the window. You can open this program from the Start menu, or just double-click a folder to open its window and view its contents.

QUICK TIP
You can also start Windows Explorer by clicking the Windows Explorer button on the taskbar.

• **Understand file addresses**

A window also contains an **Address bar**, an area just below the title bar that shows the location, or address, of the files that appear in the File list. An **address** is a sequence of folder names separated by the ▸ symbol that describes a file's location in the file hierarchy. An address shows the folder with the highest hierarchy level on the left and steps through each hierarchy level toward the right, sometimes called a **path**. For example, the My Documents folder might contain a subfolder named Notes. In this case, the Address bar would show My Documents ▸ Notes. Each location between the ▸ symbols represents a level in the file hierarchy.

• **Navigate upward and downward using the Address bar and File list**

You can use the Address bar and the File list to move up or down in the hierarchy one or more levels at a time. To **navigate upward** in your computer's hierarchy, you can click a folder or subfolder name in the Address bar. For example, in Figure B-2, you would move up in the hierarchy by clicking once on Users in the Address bar. Then the File list would show the subfolders and files inside the Users folder. To **navigate downward** in the hierarchy, double-click a subfolder in the File list. The path in the Address bar then shows the path to that subfolder.

QUICK TIP
Remember that you single-click a folder or subfolder in the Address bar to show its contents. But in the File list, you double-click a subfolder to open it.

• **Navigate upward and downward using the Navigation pane**

You can also use the Navigation pane to navigate among folders. Move the mouse pointer over the Navigation pane, then click the small triangles or to the left of a folder name to show ▷ or hide ◢ the folder's contents under the folder name. Subfolders appear indented under the folders that contain them, showing that they are inside that folder. Figure B-2 shows a folder named Users in the Navigation pane. The subfolders Katharine, Public, and Your User Name are inside the Users folder.

FIGURE B-1: Sample folder and file hierarchy

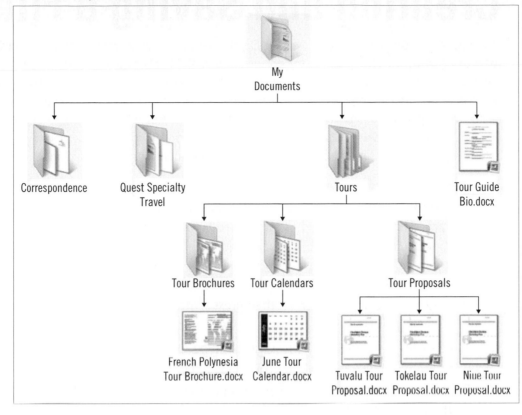

FIGURE B-2: Windows Explorer window

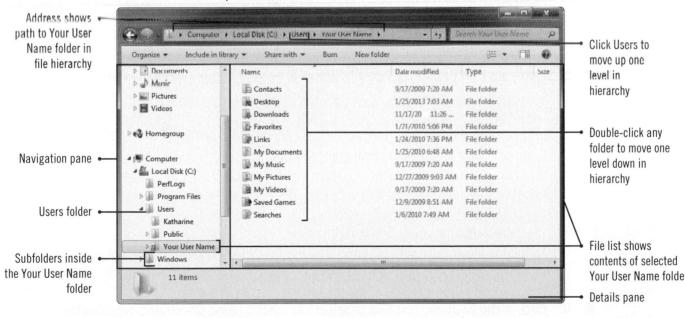

Address shows path to Your User Name folder in file hierarchy

Navigation pane

Users folder

Subfolders inside the Your User Name folder

Click Users to move up one level in hierarchy

Double-click any folder to move one level down in hierarchy

File list shows contents of selected Your User Name folder

Details pane

Plan your file organization

As you manage your files, you should plan how you want to organize them. First, identify the types of files you work with, such as images, music, and reports. Think about the content, such as personal, business, clients, or projects. Then think of a folder organization that will help you find them later. For example, use subfolders in the My Pictures folder to separate family photos from business photos or to group them by year. In the My Documents folder, you might group personal files in one subfolder and business files in another subfolder. Then create additional subfolders to further separate sets of files. You can always move files among folders and rename folders. You should periodically reevaluate your folder structure to make sure that it continues to meet your needs.

Understanding File Management

Creating and Saving a File

After you start a program and create a new file, the file exists only in your computer's **random access memory (RAM)**, which is a temporary storage location. RAM only contains information when your computer is on. When you turn off your computer, it automatically clears the contents of RAM. So you need to save a new file onto a storage device that permanently stores the file so that you can open, change, and use it later. One important storage device is your computer's hard disk built into your computer. Another popular option is a **USB flash drive**, a small, portable storage device. ▓▓▓▓ Evelyn asks you to use the WordPad accessory program to create a short summary of an Oceania tour planning meeting and save it.

STEPS

1. **Start Windows if necessary, click the** Start button ⊕ **on the taskbar, point to** All Programs, **click** Accessories, **then click** WordPad

   The WordPad program opens. Near the top of the screen you see the Ribbon containing command buttons, similar to those you used in Paint in Unit A. The Home tab appears in front. A new, blank document appears in the document window. The blinking insertion point shows you where the next character you type will appear.

2. **Type** Meeting Notes, October 11, **then press** [Enter]

   WordPad inserts a new blank line and places the insertion point at the beginning of the next line.

   > **TROUBLE**
   > If you make a typing mistake, press [Backspace] to delete the character to the left of the insertion point.

3. **Type** The 2013 tour will visit:, **press** [Enter], **type** Australia, **press** [Enter], **type** Micronesia, **press** [Enter], **type** New Zealand, **press** [Enter], **then type your name; see Figure B-3**

4. **Click the** WordPad button ▣▾ **on the upper-left side of the window below the title bar, then click** Save **on the WordPad menu**

   The first time you save a file using the Save button, the Save As dialog box opens. Use this dialog box to name the document file and choose a storage location for it. The Save As dialog box has many of the same elements as a Windows Explorer window, including an Address bar, a Navigation pane, and a File list. Below the Address bar, the **toolbar** contains command buttons you can click to perform actions. In the Address bar, you can see that WordPad chose the Documents library (which includes the My Documents folder) as the storage location.

   > **TROUBLE**
   > If you don't have a USB flash drive, save the document in the My Documents folder instead.

5. **Plug your USB flash drive into a USB port ▯ on your computer, if necessary**

   On a laptop computer, the USB port is on the left or right side of your computer. On a desktop computer, the USB port is on the front panel (you may need to open a small door to see it), or on the back panel.

6. **In the Navigation pane scroll bar, click the** Down scroll arrow ▾ **as needed to see Computer and any storage devices listed under it**

   Under Computer, you see the storage locations available on your computer, such as Local Disk (C:) (your hard drive) and Removable Disk (H:) (your USB drive name and letter might differ). These storage locations act like folders because you can open them and store files in them.

   > **TROUBLE**
   > If your Save As dialog box or title bar does not show the .rtf file extension, open any Windows Explorer window, click Organize in the toolbar, click Folder and search options, click the View tab, then under Files and Folders, click to remove the check mark from Hide extensions for known file types.

7. **Click the name for your USB flash drive**

   The files and folders on your USB drive, if any, appear in the File list. The Address bar shows the location where the file will be saved, which is now Computer > Removable Disk (H:) (or the name of your drive). You need to give your document a meaningful name so you can find it later.

8. ▶ **Click in the** Filename text box **to select the default name Document, type** Oceania Meeting, **compare your screen to Figure B-4, then click** Save

   The document is saved as a file on your USB flash drive. The filename Oceania Meeting.rtf appears in the title bar at the top of the window. The ".rtf" at the end of the filename is the file extension. A **file extension** is a three- or four-letter sequence, preceded by a period, that identifies the file as a particular type of document, in this case Rich Text Format, to your computer. The WordPad program creates files using the RTF format. Windows adds the .rtf file extension automatically after you click Save.

9. **Click the** Close button ☒ **on the WordPad window**

   The WordPad program closes. Your meeting minutes are now saved on your USB flash drive.

Understanding File Management

FIGURE B-3: Saving a document

WordPad button

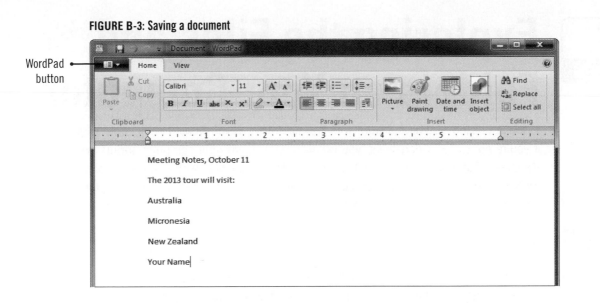

Meeting Notes, October 11

The 2013 tour will visit:

Australia

Micronesia

New Zealand

Your Name

FIGURE B-4: Save As dialog box

After you click Save, your Oceania Meeting.rtf file will be saved at this address

Toolbar

Folders on USB flash drive (your folders will differ)

Storage devices on your computer (yours will differ)

New filename

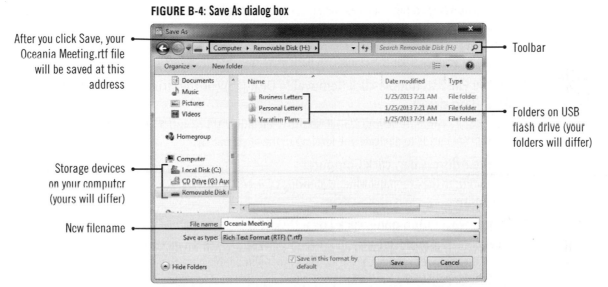

Using Windows 7 libraries

The Navigation pane contains not only files and folders, but also Libraries. A **library** gathers files and folders from different locations on your computer and displays them in one location. For example, you might have pictures in several different folders on your storage devices. You can add these folder locations to your Pictures library. Then when you want to see all your pictures, you open your Pictures library, instead of several different folders. The picture files stay in their original locations, but their names appear in the Pictures library. A library is not a folder that stores files, but rather a way of viewing similar types of documents that you have stored in multiple locations on your computer. Figure B-5 shows the four libraries that come with Windows 7: Documents, Music, Pictures, and Videos. To help you distinguish between library locations and actual folder locations, library names differ from actual folder names. For example, the My Documents folder is on your hard drive, but the library name is Documents. To add a location to a library, click the blue locations link (at the top of the File list) in the library you want to add to, click the Add button, navigate to the folder location you want to add,

then click Include folder. If you delete a file or folder from a library, you delete them from their source locations. If you delete a library, you do not delete the files in it. The Documents Library that comes with Windows already has the My Documents folder listed as a save location. So if you save a document to the Documents library, it is automatically saved to your My Documents folder.

FIGURE B-5: Libraries

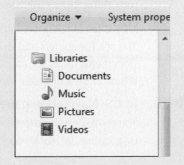

Exploring the Files and Folders on Your Computer

In the last lesson, you navigated to your USB flash drive as you worked in the Save As dialog box. But even if you're not saving a document, you will want to examine your computer and its existing folder and file structure. That way, you'll know where to save files as you work with Windows application programs. In a Windows Explorer window, you can navigate through your computer contents using the File list, the Address bar, and the Navigation pane. As you prepare for the Oceania tours, you look at the files and folders on your computer.

STEPS

TROUBLE

If you don't see the colored bar, click the More Options list arrow ▦ ▾ on the menu bar, then click Tiles.

1. **Click the Start button ⊕ on the taskbar, then click Computer**

   Your computer's storage devices appear in a window, as shown in Figure B-6, including hard drives; devices with removable storage, such as CD and DVD drives or USB flash drives; and portable devices such as personal digital assistants (PDAs). Table B-1 lists examples of different drive types. A colored bar shows you how much space has been taken up on your hard drive. You decide to move down a level in your computer's hierarchy and see what is on your USB flash drive.

TROUBLE

If you do not have a USB flash drive, click the Documents library in the Navigation pane instead.

2. **In the File list, double-click Removable Disk (H:) (or the drive name and letter for your USB flash drive)**

   You see the contents of your USB flash drive, including the Oceania Meeting.rtf file you saved in the last lesson. You decide to navigate one level up in the file hierarchy.

3. **In the Address bar, click Computer**

   You return to the Computer window showing your storage devices. You decide to look at the contents of your hard drive.

4. **In the Navigation pane, click Local Disk (C:)**

   The contents of your hard drive appear in the File list. The Users folder contains a subfolder for each user who has a user account on this computer. Recall that you double-click items in the File list to open them. In the Address bar and in the Navigation pane, you only need to single-click.

5. **In the File list, double-click the Users folder**

   You see folders for each user registered on your computer. You might see a folder with your user account name on it. Each user's folder contains that person's documents. User folder names are the log-in names that were entered when your computer was set up. When a user logs in, the computer allows that user access to the folder with the same user name. If you are using a computer with more than one user, you might not have permission to view other users' folders. There is also a Public folder that any user can open.

QUICK TIP

Click the Back button, to the left of the Address bar, to return to the window you last viewed. In the Address bar, click ▶ to the right of a folder name to see a list of the subfolders. If the folder is open, its name appears in bold.

6. **Double-click the folder with your user name on it**

   Depending on how your computer is set up, this folder might be labeled with your name; however, if you are using a computer in a lab or a public location, your folder might be called Student or Computer User or something similar. You see a list of folders, such as My Documents, My Music, and others. See Figure B-7.

7. **Double-click My Documents**

   You see the folders and documents you can open and work with. In the Address bar, the path to the My Documents folder is Computer ▶ Local Disk (C:) ▶ Users ▶ Your User Name ▶ My Documents. You decide to return to the Computer window.

8. **In the Navigation pane, click Computer**

   You moved up three levels in your hierarchy. You can also move one level up at a time in your file hierarchy by pressing the [Backspace] key on your keyboard. You once again see your computer's storage devices.

Understanding File Management

FIGURE B-6: Computer window showing storage devices

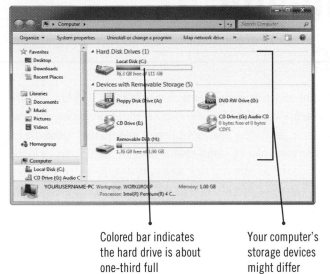

Colored bar indicates
the hard drive is about
one-third full

Your computer's
storage devices
might differ

FIGURE B-7: Your User Name folder

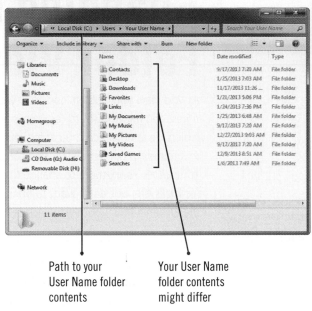

Path to your
User Name folder
contents

Your User Name
folder contents
might differ

TABLE B-1: Drive names and icons

drive type	drive icon	drive name
hard drive		C:
CD drive		Next available drive letter, such as D:
DVD drive		Next available drive letter, such as E:
USB flash drive		Next available drive letter, such as F, G:, or H:

Sharing information with homegroups and libraries

Windows 7 lets you create a **homegroup**, a named set of computers that can share information. If your computer is in a homegroup with other Windows 7 computers, you can share libraries and printers with those computers. Click Start, then click Control Panel. Under Network and Internet, click Choose homegroup and sharing options. Click to place a check mark next to the libraries and printers you want to share, then click Save changes. To share libraries that you have created on your computer with others in your homegroup, click Start, click your user name, then in the Navigation pane, click the library you want to share, click Share with on the toolbar, then click the sharing option you want, as shown in Figure B-8.

FIGURE B-8: Sharing a library

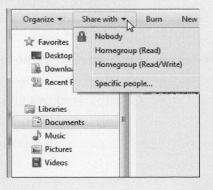

Changing File and Folder Views

As you view your folders and files, you might want to see as many items as possible in a window. At other times, you might want to see details about each item. Windows 7 lets you choose from eight different **views**, which are appearance choices for your folder contents. Each view provides different information about the files and folders in different ways. You can list your folders and files by using several different-sized icons or in lists. You can also **sort** them to change the order in which the folders and files are listed. If you want to see what a file looks like, but don't want to open the file, you can see a preview of it in the window. As you plan the Oceania tour, you review picture files in various views.

STEPS

1. **In the Navigation pane, under Libraries, click** Pictures, **then in the File list, double-click the** Sample Pictures folder

   You opened the Sample Pictures folder, which is inside your Pictures library.

2. **In the toolbar, click the** More options list arrow **next to the Change your view icon** 🖼️ ▾

   The list of available views appears in a shortcut menu. See Figure B-9.

QUICK TIP
You can also click the Change your view button 📇 ▾ (not its list arrow) repeatedly to cycle through five of the eight views.

3. **Click** Large Icons

   In this view, the pictures appear as large-sized icons in the File list, as shown in Figure B-10. For image files, this view is very helpful. You can click any view name or you can drag a slider control to move through each of the available views.

4. **Click the** Change your view More options list arrow 🖼️ ▾ **again, point to the** slider 🎚️, **then drag it so it's next to** Details

   As you drag, Live Preview shows you how each view looks in your folder. In Details view, you can see file-names, the date that files were created or modified, and other information. In Details view, you can also control the order in which the folders and files appear. In the Name column heading, you see a small triangle ⌐ Name ⌐. This indicates that the sample pictures are in alphabetical order (A, B, C,...).

QUICK TIP
Click a column heading a second time to reverse the order.

5. **Click the** Name column heading

   The items now appear in descending (Z, Y, X,...) order. The icon in the column header changes to ⌐ Name ⌐.

6. **Click the** Show the preview pane button 🖼️ **in the toolbar**

   The Preview pane opens on the right side of the screen. The **Preview pane** is an area on the right side of a window that shows you what a selected file looks like without opening it. It is especially useful for document files so you can see the first few paragraphs of a large document.

QUICK TIP
The Navigation pane also contains Favorites, which are links to folders you use frequently. To add a folder to your Favorites list, open the folder in the File list. Right-click the Favorites link in the Navigation pane, then left-click Add current location to Favorites.

7. **Click the name of your USB flash drive in the Navigation pane, then click the** Oceania Meeting.rtf **filename in the File list**

   A preview of the Oceania Meeting file you created earlier in this unit appears in the Preview pane. The Word-Pad file is not open, but you can still see its contents. The Details pane gives you information about the selected file. See Figure B-11.

8. **Click the** Hide the preview pane button 🖼️ ▾

   The Preview pane closes.

9. **Click the window's** Close button ✖️

FIGURE B-9: More options shortcut menu showing views

Slider

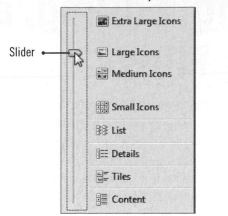

- Extra Large Icons
- Large Icons
- Medium Icons
- Small Icons
- List
- Details
- Tiles
- Content

FIGURE B-10: Sample pictures library as large icons

Your pictures might differ

FIGURE B-11: Preview of selected Oceania Meeting.rtf file

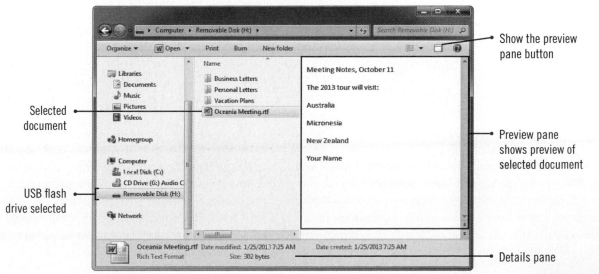

Show the preview pane button

Selected document

USB flash drive selected

Preview pane shows preview of selected document

Details pane

Understanding File Management

Opening, Editing, and Saving Files

Once you have created a file and saved it with a name in a folder on a storage device, you can easily open it and **edit** (make changes to) it. For example, you might want to add or delete text to a document, or change the color in a drawing. Then you save the file again so that it contains your latest changes. Usually you save a file with the same filename and in the same location as the original, which replaces the existing file with the latest, updated version. When you save a file you have changed, you use the Save command. Evelyn asks you to complete the meeting notes.

STEPS

1. **Click the Start button ⊕ on the taskbar, point to All Programs, click the Accessories folder, then click WordPad**

   If you use WordPad frequently, it's name might appear on the left side of the Start menu. If it does, you can click it there to open it.

2. **Click the WordPad button ▦ ▾ , then click Open**

   The Open dialog box opens. It has the same sections as the Save As dialog box and the Windows Explorer windows you used earlier in this unit. You decide to navigate to the location where you saved your Oceania Meeting.rtf file so you can open it.

   TROUBLE
   If you are not using a USB flash drive, click an appropriate storage location in the Navigation pane.

3. **Scroll down in the Navigation pane if necessary until you see Computer, then click Removable Disk (H:) (or the drive name and letter for your USB flash drive)**

   The contents of your USB flash drive appear in the File list, as shown in Figure B-12.

   QUICK TIP
   You can also double-click the filename in the File list to open the file.

4. **Click Oceania Meeting.rtf in the File list, then click Open**

   The document you created earlier opens.

5. **Click to the right of the "d" in New Zealand, press [Enter], then type Evelyn Swazey closed the meeting.**

   The edited document includes the text you just typed. See Figure B-13.

   QUICK TIP
   Instead of using the WordPad menu and Save command to save a document, you can also click the Save button. ▦ in the Quick Access toolbar at the top of the WordPad window.

6. **Click the WordPad button ▦ ▾ , then click Save, as shown in Figure B-14**

   WordPad saves the document with your most recent changes, using the filename and location you specified when you saved it for the first time. When you save an existing file, the Save As dialog box does not open.

7. **Click ▦ ▾ , then click Exit**

Comparing Save and Save As

The WordPad menu has two save command options—Save and Save As. When you first save a file, the Save As dialog box opens (whether you choose Save or Save As). Here you can select the drive and folder where you want to save the file and enter its filename. If you edit a previously saved file, you can save the file to the same location with the same filename using the Save command. The Save command updates the stored file using the same location and filename without opening the Save As dialog box. In some situations, you might want to save another copy of the existing document using a different filename or in a different storage location. To do this, open the document, use the Save As command, and then navigate to a different location, and/or edit the name of the file.

FIGURE B-12: Navigating in the Open dialog box

The folders on your
drive will differ

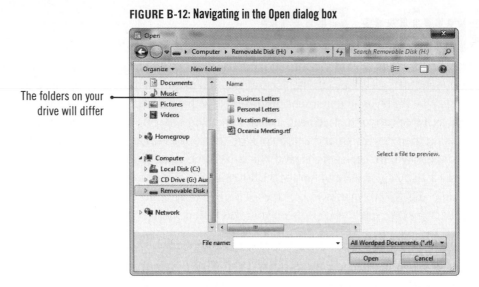

FIGURE B-13: Edited document

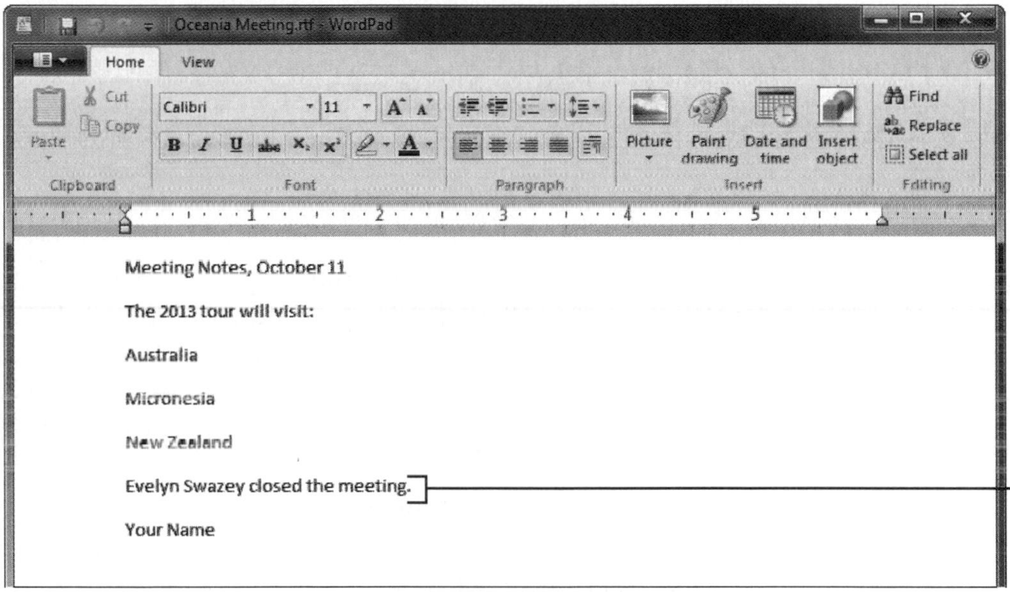

Meeting Notes, October 11

The 2013 tour will visit:

Australia

Micronesia

New Zealand

Evelyn Swazey closed the meeting.

Your Name

Added text

FIGURE B-14: Saving a revised document

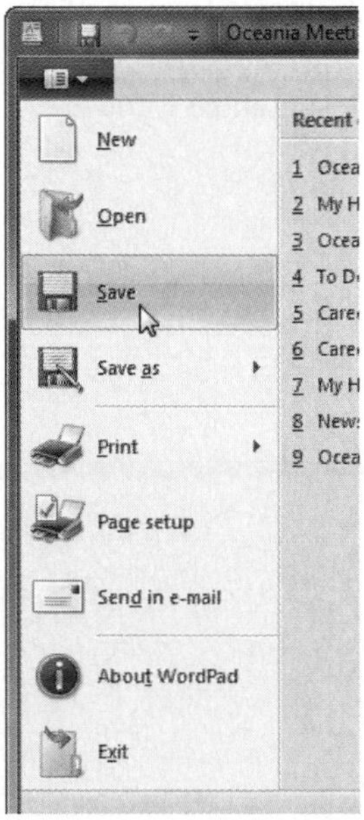

New

Open

Save

Save as

Print

Page setup

Send in e-mail

About WordPad

Exit

Recent

1 Ocea
2 My H
3 Ocea
4 To D
5 Care
6 Care
7 My H
8 New
9 Ocea

Understanding File Management

Copying Files

As you have learned, saving a file in a location on your hard drive stores it so you can open it later. But sometimes you will want to make a copy of a file. For example, you might want to put a copy on a USB flash drive so you can open the file on another machine or share a file with a friend or colleague. Or you might want to create a copy as a **backup**, or replacement, in case something happens to your original file. You copy files and folders using the Copy command and then place the copy in another location using the Paste command. You cannot have two copies of a file with the same name in the same folder. If you attempt to do this, Windows 7 will ask you if you want to replace the first one then gives you a chance to give the second copy a different name. Evelyn asks you to create a backup copy of the meeting notes document you created and paste it in a new folder you create on your USB flash drive.

STEPS

1. **Click the** Start button **on the taskbar, then click** Computer

2. **In the File list, double-click** Removable Disk (H:) **(or the drive name and letter for your USB flash drive)**
   First you create the new folder Evelyn needs.

3. **In the toolbar, click the** New folder button
   A new folder appears in the File list, with its name, New folder, selected. Because the folder name is selected, any text you type replaces the selected text as the folder name.

4. **Type** Meeting Notes, **then press** [Enter]
   You named the new folder Meeting Notes. Next, you copy your original Oceania Meeting.rtf file.

> **QUICK TIP**
> You can also copy a file by right-clicking the file in the File list and then clicking Copy. To use the keyboard, press and hold [Ctrl] and press [C], then release both keys.

5. **In the File list, click the** Oceania Meeting.rtf **document you saved earlier, click the** Organize **button on the toolbar, then click** Copy, **as shown in Figure B-15**
   When you use the Copy command, Windows 7 places a duplicate copy of the file in an area of your computer's random access memory called the **clipboard**, ready to paste, or place, in a new location. Copying and pasting a file leaves the file in its original location. The copied file remains on the clipboard until you copy something else or end your Windows 7 session.

6. **In the File list, double-click the** Meeting Notes folder
   The folder opens.

> **QUICK TIP**
> To paste using the keyboard, press and hold [Ctrl] and press [V], then release both keys.

7. **Click the** Organize **button on the toolbar, then click** Paste
   A copy of your Oceania Meeting.rtf file is pasted into your new Meeting Notes folder. See Figure B-16. You now have two copies of the Oceania Meeting.rtf file: one on your USB flash drive in the main folder, and a copy of the file in a folder called Meeting Notes on your USB flash drive. The file remains on the clipboard so you can paste it again to other locations if you like.

Understanding File Management

FIGURE B-15: Copying a file

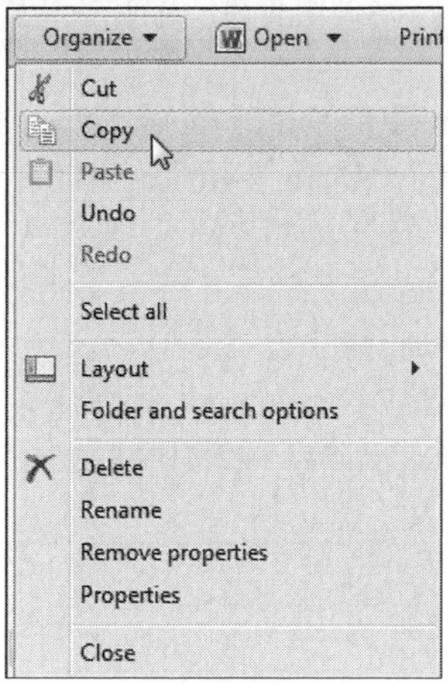

FIGURE B-16: Duplicate file pasted into Meeting Notes folder

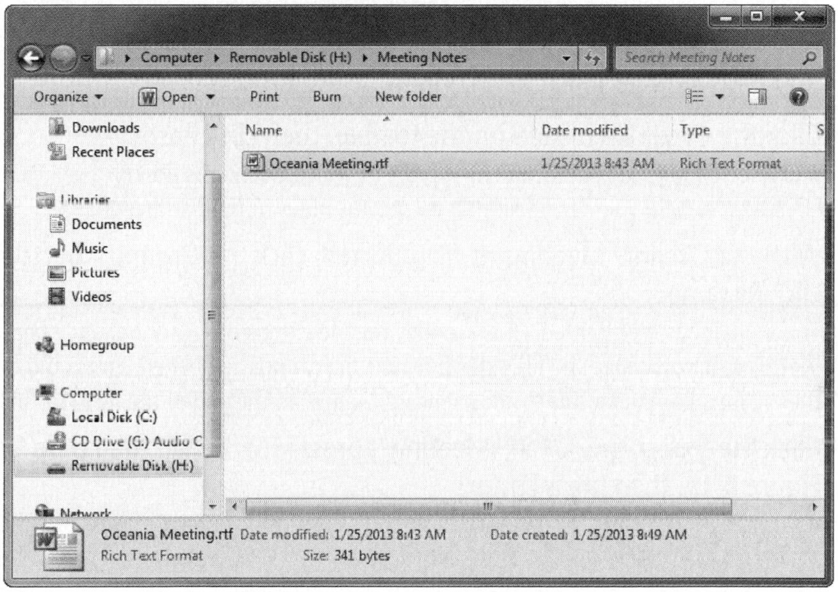

Copying files using Send to

You can also copy and paste a file to an external storage device using the Send to command. In a window, right-click the file you want to copy, point to Send to, then in the shortcut menu, click the name of the device where you want to send a copy of the file. This leaves the original file on your hard drive and creates a copy on the external device, all with just one command. See Table B-2 for a short summary of other shortcut menu commands.

TABLE B-2: Selected Send to menu commands

menu option	use to	menu option	use to
Compressed (zipped) folder	Create a new compressed (smaller) file with a .zip file extension	Documents	Copy the file to the Documents library
Desktop (create shortcut)	Create a shortcut (link) for the file on the desktop	DVD RW Drive (D:)	Copy the file to your computer's DVD drive
Mail recipient	Create an e-mail with the file attached to it (only if you have an e-mail program on your computer)	Removable Disk (H:)	Copy the file to your removable disk (H:)

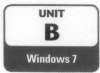

UNIT
B
Windows 7

Moving and Renaming Files

As you work with files, you might need to move files or folders to another location. You can move one or more files or folders. You might move them to a different folder on the same drive or a different drive. When you **move** a file, the file is transferred to the new location and no longer exists in its original location. You can move a file using the Cut and Paste commands. After you create a file, you might find that the original name you gave the file isn't clear anymore, so you can rename it to make it more descriptive or accurate. ▰▰▰▰ You decide to move your original Oceania Meeting.rtf document to your Documents library. After you move it, you decide to edit the filename so it better describes the file contents.

STEPS

QUICK TIP

You can also cut a file by right-clicking the file in the File list and then clicking Cut. To use the keyboard, press and hold [Ctrl] and press [X], then release both keys.

QUICK TIP

You can also paste a file by right-clicking an empty area in the File list and then clicking Paste. To use the keyboard, press and hold [Ctrl] and press [V], then release both keys.

1. **In the Address bar, click Removable Disk (H:) (or the drive name and letter for your USB flash drive)**

2. **Click the Oceania Meeting.rtf document to select it**

▶ 3. **Click the Organize button on the toolbar, then click Cut**

   The icon representing the cut file becomes lighter in color, indicating you have cut it, as shown in Figure B-17. You navigate to your Documents library, in preparation for pasting the cut document there.

4. **In the Navigation Pane, under Libraries, click Documents**

▶ 5. **Click the Organize button on the toolbar, then click Paste**

   The Oceania Meeting.rtf document appears in your Documents library. See Figure B-18. The filename could be clearer, to help you remember that it contains notes from your meeting.

6. **With the Oceania Meeting.rtf file selected, click the Organize button on the toolbar, then click Rename**

   The filename is highlighted. In a window, the file extension cannot change because it identifies the file to WordPad. If you delete the file extension, the file cannot be opened. You could type a new name to replace the old one, but you decide to add the word "Notes" to the end of the filename instead.

7. **Click the I after the "g" in "Meeting", press [Spacebar], then type Notes, as shown in Figure B-19, then press [Enter]**

   You changed the name of the document copy in the Documents library. The filename now reads Oceania Meeting Notes.rtf.

8. **Close the window**

Understanding File Management

FIGURE B-17: Cutting a file

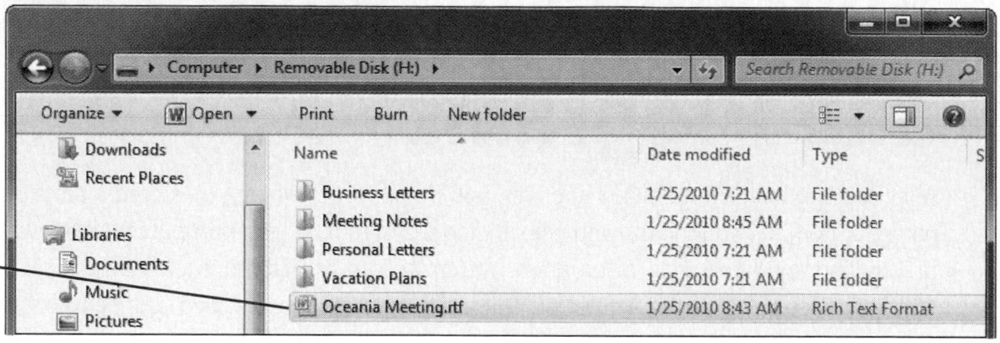

Computer ▸ Removable Disk (H:) ▸

Search Removable Disk (H:)

Organize ▾   W Open ▾   Print   Burn   New folder

Downloads
Recent Places

Libraries
Documents
Music
Pictures

Name	Date modified	Type	S
Business Letters	1/25/2010 7:21 AM	File folder	
Meeting Notes	1/25/2010 8:45 AM	File folder	
Personal Letters	1/25/2010 7:21 AM	File folder	
Vacation Plans	1/25/2010 7:21 AM	File folder	
Oceania Meeting.rtf	1/25/2010 8:43 AM	Rich Text Format	

Icon is lighter, indicating you have cut the file

FIGURE B-18: Pasted file in Documents library

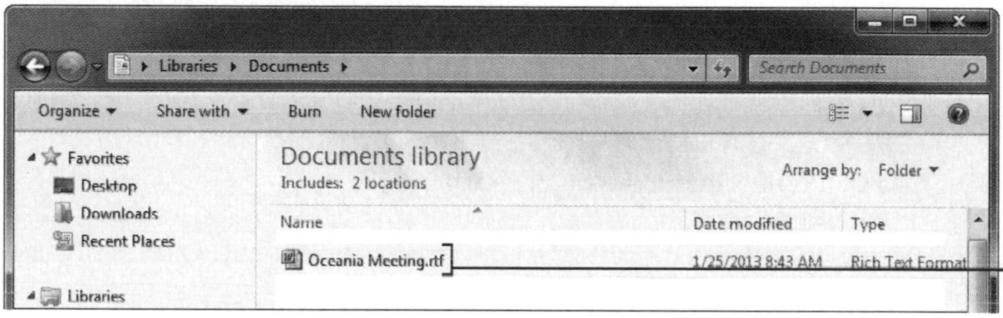

Libraries ▸ Documents ▸

Search Documents

Organize ▾   Share with ▾   Burn   New folder

Favorites
Desktop
Downloads
Recent Places

Libraries

Documents library
Includes: 2 locations

Arrange by: Folder ▾

Name	Date modified	Type
Oceania Meeting.rtf	1/25/2013 8:43 AM	Rich Text Format

Pasted file

FIGURE B-19: Renaming a file

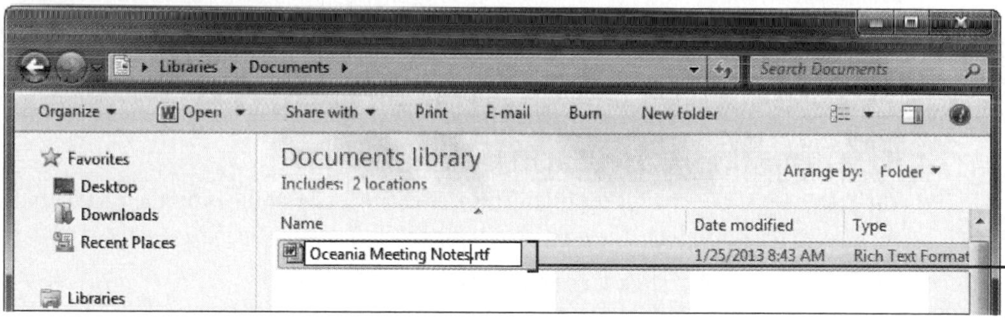

Libraries ▸ Documents ▸

Search Documents

Organize ▾   W Open ▾   Share with ▾   Print   E-mail   Burn   New folder

Favorites
Desktop
Downloads
Recent Places

Libraries

Documents library
Includes: 2 locations

Arrange by: Folder ▾

Name	Date modified	Type
Oceania Meeting Notes.rtf	1/25/2013 8:43 AM	Rich Text Format

Renamed file

Using drag and drop to copy or move files to new locations

You can also use the mouse to copy a file and place the copy in a new location. **Drag and drop** is a technique in which you use your pointing device to drag a file or folder into a different folder and then drop it, or let go of the mouse button, to place it in that folder. Using drag and drop does not copy your file to the clipboard. If you drag and drop a file to a folder on another drive, Windows *copies* the file. See Figure B-20. However, if you drag and drop a file to a folder on the same drive, Windows 7 *moves* the file into that folder instead. If you want to move a file to another drive, hold down [Shift] while you drag and drop. If you want to copy a file to another folder on the same drive, hold down [Ctrl] while you drag and drop.

FIGURE B-20: Copying a file using drag and drop

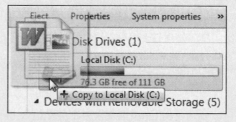

Eject   Properties   System properties   »

Disk Drives (1)

Local Disk (C:)

76.3 GB free of 111 GB

Copy to Local Disk (C:)

Devices with Removable Storage (5)

Searching for Files, Folders, and Programs

After copying or moving folders and files, you might forget where you stored a particular folder or file, its name, or both. Or you might need help finding a program on your computer. **Windows Search** helps you quickly find any file, folder, or program. You must type one or more letter sequences or words that help Windows 7 identify the item you want. The search text you type is called your **search criteria**. Your search criteria can be a filename, part of a filename, or any other characters you choose. Windows 7 will find files with that information in its name or with that information inside the file. For example, if you type "word," Windows 7 will find the program Microsoft Word, any documents with "word" in its title, or any document with "word" inside the file. To search your entire computer, including its attached drives, you can use the Search box on the Start menu. To search within a particular folder, you can use the Search box in a Windows Explorer window. ▓▓▓▓▓ You want to locate the copy of the Oceania Meeting Notes.rtf document so you can print it for a colleague.

STEPS

1. Click the Start button ⊕ on the taskbar

The Search programs and files box at the bottom of the Start menu already contains the insertion point, ready for you to type search criteria. You begin your search by typing a part of a word that is in the filename.

2. Type me

Even before you finish typing the word "meeting", the Start menu lists all programs, files, and Control Panel items that have the letters "me" in their title or somewhere inside the file or the file properties. See Figure B-21. Your search results will differ, depending on the programs and files on your computer. **File properties** are details that Windows stores about a file. Windows arranges the search results into categories.

> **QUICK TIP**
> Search text is not case sensitive. Typing lowercase "mee", you will still find items that start with "Mee" or "mee".

3. Type e

The search results narrow to only the files that contain "mee". The search results become more specific every time you add more text to your criteria finding the two versions of your meeting notes file. See Figure B-22.

4. Point to the Oceania Meeting.rtf filename under Files

The ScreenTip shows the file location. This Oceania Meeting.rtf file is on the USB flash drive. The filenames are links to the document. You only need to single-click a file to open it.

> **TROUBLE**
> Your file might open in another program on your computer that reads RTF files. You can continue with the lesson.

5. Under Documents, click Oceania Meeting Notes.rtf

The file opens in WordPad.

6. Click the Close button ▨▨▨ in the program window's title bar

You can search in a folder or on a drive using the search box in any Windows Explorer window.

> **TROUBLE**
> If you do not have a USB flash drive, click another storage location in the Navigation pane.

7. Click ⊕, click Computer, in the Navigation pane click Removable Disk (H:) (or the drive name and letter for your USB flash drive)

8. Click the Search Removable Disk (H:) text box, to the right of the Address bar

9. Type mee to list all files and folders on your USB flash drive that contain "mee"

The search criterion, mee, is highlighted in the filenames. The results include the folder called Meeting Notes and the file named Oceania Meeting.rtf. Because you navigated to your USB flash drive, Windows only lists the document version that is on that drive. See Figure B-23.

10. Double-click Oceania Meeting.rtf in the File list to open the document file in WordPad, view the file, close WordPad, then close the Windows Explorer window

FIGURE B-21: Searching on criterion "me"

FIGURE B-22: Searching on criterion "mee"

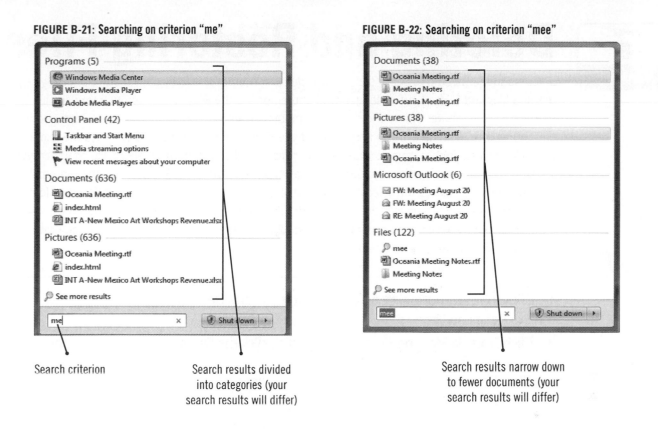

Search criterion

Search results divided into categories (your search results will differ)

Search results narrow down to fewer documents (your search results will differ)

FIGURE B-23: Searching using the Search Computer text box in folder window

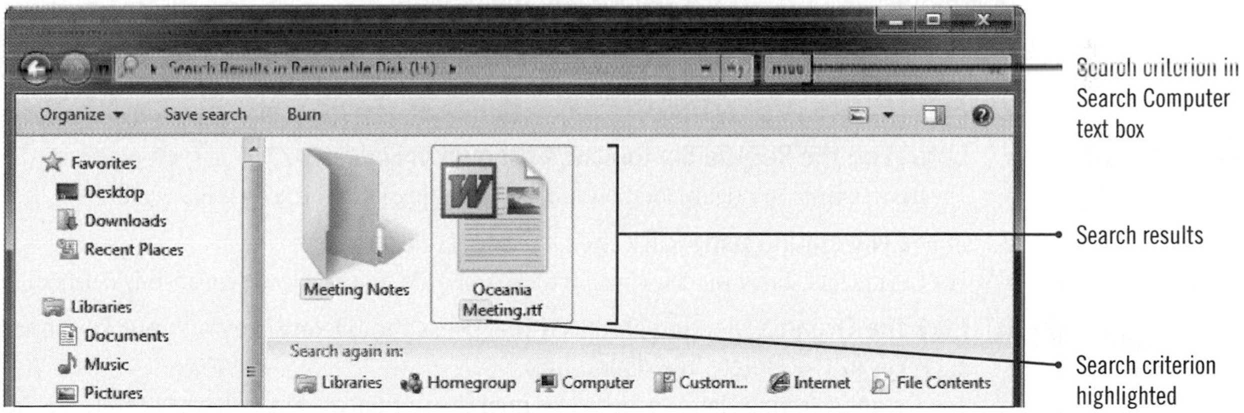

Search criterion in Search Computer text box

Search results

Search criterion highlighted

Performing more advanced searches

To locate all files that have the same file extension (such as .rtf), type the file extension as your search criterion. If you want to locate files created by a certain person, use the first name, last name, or first and last name as your search criteria. If you want to locate files created on a certain date, type the date (for example, 7/9/2012) as your search criterion. If you remember the title in a document, type the title as your search criterion. If you have created e-mail contacts in your Contacts folder, you can type the person's name to find his or her e-mail address.

UNIT
B
Windows 7

Deleting and Restoring Files

If you no longer need a folder or file, you can delete (or remove) it from the storage device. By regularly deleting files and folders you no longer need and emptying the Recycle Bin, you free up valuable storage space on your computer. This also keeps your computer uncluttered. Windows 7 places folders and files you delete from your hard drive in the Recycle Bin. If you delete a folder, Windows 7 removes the folder as well as all files and subfolders stored in it. If you later discover that you need a deleted file or folder, you can restore it to its original location, but only if you have not yet emptied the Recycle Bin. Emptying the Recycle Bin permanently removes the deleted folders and files from your computer. However, files and folders you delete from a removable drive, such as a USB flash drive, do not go to the Recycle Bin. They are immediately and permanently deleted and cannot be restored. ▰▰▰▰ You delete the meeting notes copy saved in the Documents library and then restore it.

STEPS

1. **Click the Start button 🌐 on the taskbar, then click Documents**

   Your Documents library opens.

2. **Click Oceania Meeting Notes.rtf to select it, click the Organize button on the toolbar, then click Delete**

   The Delete File dialog box opens so you can confirm the deletion, as shown in Figure B-24.

3. **Click Yes**

   You deleted the file from the Documents library. Windows moved it into the Recycle Bin.

   > **QUICK TIP**
   > If the Recycle Bin icon does not contain crumpled paper, then it is empty.

4. **Click the Minimize button 🗕 on the window's title bar and examine the Recycle Bin icon**

   The Recycle Bin icon appears to contain crumpled paper. This tells you that the Recycle Bin contains deleted folders and files.

5. **Double-click the Recycle Bin icon on the desktop**

   The Recycle Bin window opens and displays any previously deleted folders and files, including the Oceania Meeting Notes.rtf file.

   > **QUICK TIP**
   > To delete a file completely in one action, click the file to select it, press and hold [Shift], then press [Delete]. A message will ask if you want to permanently delete the file. If you click Yes, Windows deletes the file without sending it to the Recycle Bin. Use caution, however, because you cannot restore the file.

6. **Click the Oceania Meeting Notes.rtf file to select it, then click the Restore this item button on the Recycle Bin toolbar, as shown in Figure B-25**

   The file returns to its original location and no longer appears in the Recycle Bin window.

7. **In the Navigation pane, click the Documents library**

   The Documents library window contains the restored file. You decide to permanently delete this file.

8. **Click the Oceania Meeting Notes.rtf file, press the [Delete] key on your keyboard, then click Yes in the Delete File dialog box**

   The Oceania Meeting Notes.rtf file moves from the Documents library to the Recycle Bin. You decide to permanently delete all documents in the Recycle Bin.

   NOTE: If you are using a computer that belongs to someone else, or that is in a computer lab, make sure you have permission to empty the Recycle Bin before proceeding with the next step.

9. **Minimize the window, double-click the Recycle Bin, click the Empty the Recycle Bin button on the toolbar, click Yes in the dialog box, then close all open windows**

Understanding File Management

FIGURE B-24: Delete File dialog box

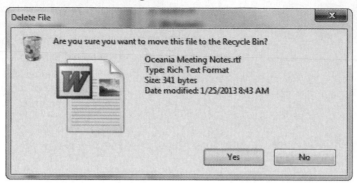

FIGURE B-25: Restoring a file from the Recycle Bin

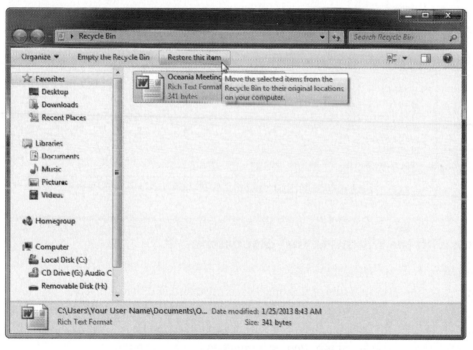

Selecting more than one file

You might want to select a group of files or folders in order to cut, copy, or delete them all at once. To select a group of items that are next to each other in a window, click the first item in the group, press and hold [Shift], then click the last item in the group. Both items you click and all the items between them become selected. To select files that are not next to each other, click the first file, press and hold [Ctrl], then click the other items you want to select as a group. Then you can copy, cut, or delete the group of files or folders you selected.

Practice

For current SAM information, including versions and content details, visit SAM Central (http://samcentral.course.com). If you have a SAM user profile, you may have access to hands-on instruction, practice, and assessment of the skills covered in this unit. Since various versions of SAM are supported throughout the life of this text, check with your instructor for the correct instructions and URL/Web site for accessing assignments.

Concepts Review

Label the elements of the Windows 7 window shown in Figure B-26.

FIGURE B-26

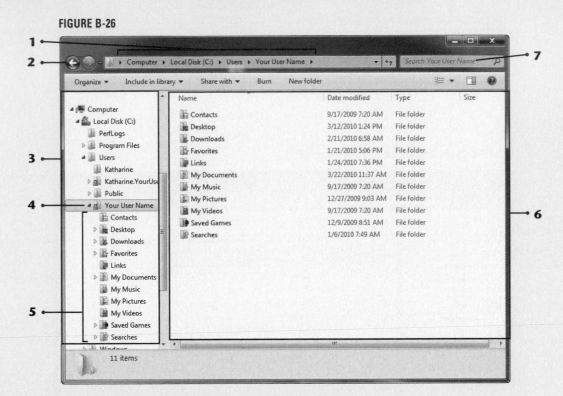

Match each term with the statement that best describes it.

8. File management	a. Shows file's path
9. File extension	b. Structure of files and folders organized in different levels
10. Address bar	c. Describes a file's location in the file hierarchy
11. Path	d. Skills that help you organize your files and folders
12. Library	e. Contains buttons in a Windows Explorer window
13. Toolbar	f. A three- or four-letter sequence, preceded by a period, that identifies the type of file
14. File hierarchy	g. Gathers files and folders from different computer locations

Select the best answer from the list of choices.

15. The way your files appear in the Details window is determined by the:
   a. Path.
   b. View.
   c. Subfolder.
   d. Criterion.

16. When you move a file:
   a. It remains in its original location.
   b. It is no longer in its original location.
   c. It is copied to another location.
   d. It is no longer in your file hierarchy.

17. The text you type in the Search programs and files box on the Start menu is called:
   a. Search criteria.
   b. RAM.
   c. Sorting.
   d. Clipboard.

18. Which of the following is not a window section?

a. Address bar

b. File list

c. Navigation pane

d. Clipboard

19. Which part of a window lets you see a file's contents without opening the file?

a. File list

b. Preview pane

c. Navigation pane

d. Address bar

20. In a file hierarchy, a folder inside another folder is called a:

a. Subfolder.

b. Internal hard disk.

c. Clipboard.

d. Path.

21. After you delete a file from your hard disk, it is automatically placed in the:

a. USB flash drive.

b. Clipboard.

c. Recycle bin.

d. Search box.

22. When you copy a file, it is automatically placed on the:

a. Preview pane.

b. My Documents folder.

c. Hierarchy.

d. Clipboard.

Skills Review

1. Understand folders and files.

a. Assume that you sell books as a home business. How would you organize your folders and files using a file hierarchy? How would you use folders and subfolders? Draw a diagram and write a short paragraph explaining your answer.

2. Create and save a file.

a. Connect your USB flash drive to a USB port on your computer, then open WordPad from the All Programs menu.

b. Type **Marketing Plan: Oceania Tours** as the title, then start a new line.

c. Type your name, then press [Enter] twice.

d. Create the following list:

Brochures

Direct e-mail

Web ads

Travel conventions

e. Save the WordPad file with the filename **Oceania Marketing Plan.rtf** on your USB flash drive.

f. View the filename in the WordPad title bar, then close WordPad.

3. Explore the files and folders on your computer.

a. Open a Windows Explorer window that shows the contents of your computer.

b. Use the File list to navigate to your USB flash drive. (If you do not have a USB flash drive, navigate to your Documents library using the Navigation pane.)

c. Use the Address bar to navigate to Computer again.

d. Use the Navigation pane to navigate to your hard drive.

e. Use the File list to open the Users folder, and then open the folder that represents your user name.

f. Open the My Documents folder. (*Hint*: The path is Local Disk (C:) ▶ Users ▶ [Your User Name] ▶ My Documents.)

g. Use the Navigation pane to navigate back to your computer contents.

4. Change file and folder views.

a. Navigate to your USB flash drive using the method of your choice.

b. View its contents as large icons.

c. Use the View slider to view the drive contents in all the other seven views.

d. Use the Change your view button to cycle through the five available views.

e. Open the Preview pane, then click a file and view its preview. Repeat with two more files.

f. Close the Preview pane.

Skills Review (continued)

5. **Open, edit, and save files.**
   a. Open WordPad.
   b. Use the Open dialog box to open the Oceania Marketing Plan.rtf document you created.
   c. After the text "Travel conventions," add a line with the text **Canadian magazines**.
   d. Save the document and close WordPad.

6. **Copy files.**
   a. In the Windows Explorer window, navigate to your USB flash drive if necessary.
   b. Copy the Oceania Marketing Plan.rtf document.
   c. Create a new folder named **Marketing** on your USB flash drive, then open the folder. (If you don't have a USB flash drive, create the folder in your Documents library.)
   d. Paste the document copy in the new folder.

7. **Move and rename files.**
   a. Navigate to your USB flash drive.
   b. Select the original Oceania Marketing Plan.rtf document, then cut it.
   c. Navigate to your Documents library and paste the file there.
   d. Rename the file **Oceania Marketing Plan - Backup.rtf**.

8. **Search for files, folders, and programs.**
   a. Use the Search programs and files box on the Start menu to enter the search criterion **ma**.
   b. Change your search criterion so it reads **mar**.
   c. Open the backup copy of your Oceania Marketing Plan document from the Start menu, then close WordPad.
   d. In Windows Explorer, navigate to your Documents library, then use the criterion **mar** in the Search Documents box.
   e. Open the backup copy of the Oceania Marketing Plan document from the File list, then close WordPad.

9. **Delete and restore files.**
   a. Navigate to your Documents library if necessary.
   b. Delete the Oceania Marketing Plan - Backup.rtf file.
   c. Open the Recycle Bin, and restore the document to its original location, navigate to your Documents library, then move the Oceania Marketing Plan - Backup file to your USB flash drive.

Independent Challenge 1

To meet the needs of pet owners in your town, you have opened a pet-sitting business named PetCare. Customers hire you to care for their pets in their own homes when the pet owners go on vacation. To promote your new business, you want to develop a newspaper ad and a flyer.

a. Connect your USB flash drive to your computer, if necessary.
b. Create a new folder named **PetCare** on your USB flash drive.
c. In the PetCare folder, create two subfolders named **Advertising** and **Flyers**.
d. Use WordPad to create a short ad for your local newspaper that describes your business:
   - Use the name of the business as the title for your document.
   - Write a short paragraph about the business. Include a fictitious location, street address, and phone number.
   - After the paragraph, type your name.
e. Save the WordPad document with the filename **Newspaper Ad** in the Advertising folder, then close the document and exit WordPad.
f. Open a Windows Explorer window, and navigate to the Advertising folder.
g. View the contents in at least three different views, then choose the view option that you prefer.
h. Copy the Newspaper Ad.rtf file, and paste a copy in the Flyers folder.
i. Rename the copy **Newspaper Ad Backup.rtf**.
j. Close the folder.

Independent Challenge 2

As a freelance editor for several national publishers, you depend on your computer to meet critical deadlines. Whenever you encounter a computer problem, you contact a computer consultant who helps you resolve the problem. This consultant asked you to document, or keep records of, your computer's current settings.

a. Connect your USB flash drive to your computer, if necessary.

b. Open the Computer window so that you can view information on your drives and other installed hardware.

c. View the window contents using three different views, then choose the one you prefer.

d. Open WordPad and create a document with the title **My Hardware Documentation** and your name on separate lines.

e. List the names of the hard drive (or drives), devices with removable storage, and any other hardware devices, installed on the computer you are using. Also include the total size and amount of free space on your hard drive(s) and removable storage drive(s). (*Hint*: If you need to check the Computer window for this information, use the taskbar button for the Computer window to view your drives, then use the WordPad taskbar button to return to WordPad.)

Advanced Challenge Exercise

- Navigate your computer's file hierarchy, and determine its various levels.
- On paper, draw a diagram showing your file hierarchy, starting with Computer at the top, and going down at least four levels if available.

f. Save the WordPad document with the filename **My Hardware Documentation** on your USB flash drive.

g. Preview your document, print your WordPad document, then close WordPad.

Independent Challenge 3

You are an attorney at Lopez, Rickland, and Willgor, a large law firm. You participate in your firm's community outreach program by speaking at career days in area high schools. You teach students about career opportunities available in the field of law. You want to create a folder structure on your USB flash drive to store the files for each session.

a. Connect your USB flash drive to your computer, then open the window for your USB flash drive.

b. Create a folder named **Career Days**.

c. In the Career Days folder, create a subfolder named **Mather High**.

Advanced Challenge Exercise

- In the Mather High folder, create subfolders named **Class Outline** and **Visual Aids**.
- Rename the Visual Aids folder **Class Handouts**.
- Create a new folder named **Interactive Presentations** in the Class Handouts subfolder.

d. Close the Mather High window.

e. Use WordPad to create a document with the title **Career Areas** and your name on separate lines, and the following list of items:

Current Opportunities:
Attorney
Corrections Officer
Forensic Scientist
Paralegal
Judge

f. Save the WordPad document with the filename **Careers Listing.rtf** in the Mather High folder. (*Hint:* After you switch to your USB flash drive in the Save As dialog box, open the Career Days folder, then open the Mather High folder before saving the file.)

g. Close WordPad.

Independent Challenge 3 (continued)

h. Open WordPad and the Careers Listing document again, then add **Court Reporter** to the bottom of the list, then save the file and close WordPad.

i. Using pencil and paper, draw a diagram of your new folder structure.

j. Use the Start menu to search your computer using the search criterion **car**. Locate the Careers Listing.rtf document in the list, and use the link to open the file.

k. Close the file.

Real Life Independent Challenge

Think of a hobby or volunteer activity that you do now, or one that you would like to do. You will use your computer to help you manage your plans or ideas for this activity.

a. Using paper and a pencil, sketch a folder structure using at least two subfolders that you could create on your USB flash drive to contain your documents for this activity.

b. Connect your USB flash drive to your computer, then open the window for your USB flash drive.

c. Create the folder structure for your activity, using your sketch as a reference.

d. Think of at least three tasks that you can do to further your work in your chosen activity.

e. Open WordPad and create a document with the title **Next Steps** at the top of the page and your name on the next line.

f. List the three tasks, then save the file in one of the folders you created on your USB flash drive, using the title **To Do.rtf**.

g. Close WordPad, then open a Windows Explorer window for the folder where you stored the document.

h. Create a copy of the file, give the copy a new name, then place a copy of the document in your Documents library.

i. Delete the document copy from your Documents library.

j. Open the Recycle Bin window, and restore the document to the Documents library.

Visual Workshop

You are a technical support specialist at Emergency Services. The company supplies medical staff members to hospital emergency rooms in Los Angeles. You need to respond to your company's employee questions quickly and thoroughly. You decide that it is time to evaluate and reorganize the folder structure on your computer. That way, you'll be able to respond more quickly to staff requests. Create the folder structure shown in Figure B-27 on your USB flash drive. As you work, use WordPad to prepare a simple outline of the steps you follow to create the folder structure. Add your name to the document, and store it in an appropriate location.

FIGURE B-27

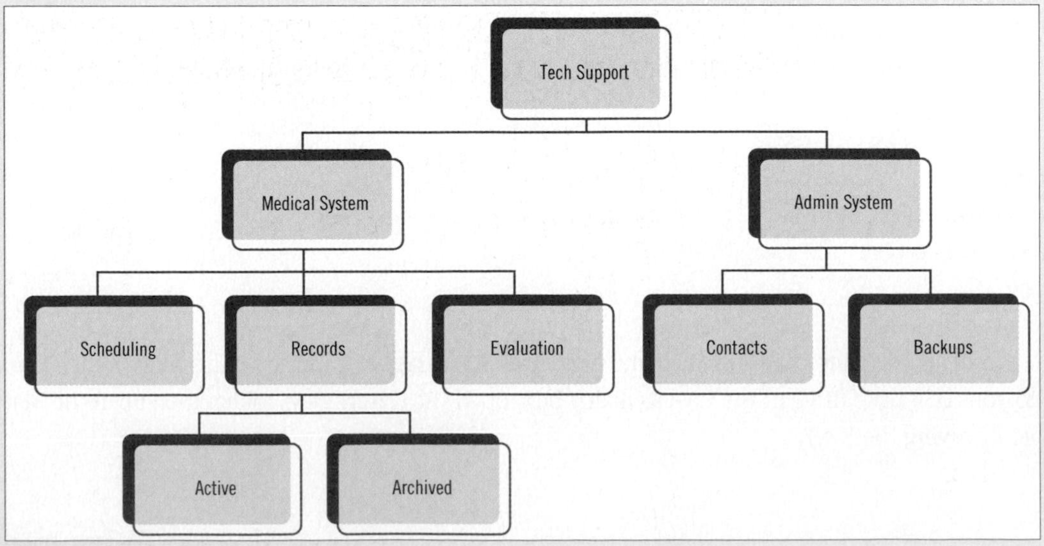

Understanding File Management

Glossary

Accessories Simple Windows programs that perform specific tasks, such as the Calculator accessory for performing calculations.

Active window The window you are currently using; if multiple windows are open, the window with the darker title bar.

Address A sequence of drive and folder names that describes a folder's or file's location in the file hierarchy; the highest hierarchy level is on the left, with lower hierarchy levels separated by the ▶ symbol to its right.

Address bar In a window, the white area just below the title bar that shows the file hierarchy, or address of the files that appear in the file list below it; the address appears as a series of links (separated by the ▶ symbol) you can click to navigate to other locations on your computer.

Aero A Windows 7 viewing option that shows windows as translucent objects and features subtle animations; only available on a computer that has enough memory to support Aero and on which a Windows Aero theme has been selected.

Aero Flip 3D A Windows 7 feature that lets you preview all open folders and documents without using the taskbar and that displays open windows in a stack if you press [Ctrl][🪟][Tab]; only available if using a Windows Aero theme.

Aero Peek A Windows 7 feature that lets you point to a taskbar icon representing an open program and see a thumbnail (small version) of the open file; only visible if the computer uses a Windows Aero theme.

Application program Any program that lets you work with files or create and edit files such as graphics, letters, financial summaries, and other useful documents, as well as view Web pages on the Internet and send and receive e-mail.

Backup A duplicate copy of a file that is stored in another location.

Border A window's edge; drag to resize the window.

Canvas In the Paint accessory program, the area in the center of the program window that you use to create drawings.

Case sensitive Describes a program's ability to differentiate between uppercase and lowercase letters; usually used to describe how an operating system evaluates passwords that users type to gain entry to user accounts.

Check box A box that turns an option on when checked or off when unchecked.

Click To quickly press and release the left button on the pointing device; also called single-click.

Clipboard A location in a computer's random access memory that stores information you copy or cut.

Close button In a Windows title bar, the rightmost button; closes the open window, program, and/or document.

Command An instruction to perform a task, such as opening a file or emptying the Recycle Bin.

Command button A button you click to issue instructions to modify program objects.

Copy To make a duplicate copy of a file, folder, or other object that you want to store in another location.

Default In a program window or dialog box, a value that is already set by the program; you can change the default to any valid value.

Desktop A shaded or picture background that appears to fill the screen after a computer starts up; usually contains icons, which are small images that represent items on your computer and allow you to interact with the computer.

Desktop background The shaded area behind your desktop objects; can show colors, designs, or photographs, which you can customize.

Details pane A pane located at the bottom of a window that displays information about the selected disk, drive, folder, or file.

Device A hardware component that is part of your computer system, such as a disk drive or a pointing device.

Dialog box A window with controls that lets you tell Windows how you want to complete a program command.

Document window The portion of a program window in which you create the document; displays all or part of an open document.

Documents folder The folder on your hard drive used to store most of the files you create or receive from others; might contain subfolders to organize the files into smaller groups.

Double-click To quickly press and release or click the left button on the pointing device twice.

Drag To point to an object, press and hold the left button on the pointing device, move the object to a new location, and then release the left button.

Drag and drop To use a pointing device to move or copy a file or folder to a new location.

Drive A physical location on your computer where you can store files.

Drive name A name for a drive that consists of a letter followed by a colon, such as C: for the hard disk drive.

Edit To make changes to a file.

File A collection of information stored on your computer, such as a letter, video, or program.

File extension A three- or four-letter sequence, preceded by a period, at the end of a filename that identifies the file as a particular type of document; documents in the Rich Text Format have the file extension .rtf.

File hierarchy The tree-like structure of folders and files on your computer.

File list In Windows Explorer, the right section of the window; shows the contents of the folder selected in the Navigation pane on the left.

File management The ability to organize folders and files on your computer.

Filename A unique, descriptive name for a file that identifies the file's content.

File properties Details that Windows stores about a file, such as the date it was created or modified.

Folder An electronic container that helps you organize your computer files, like a cardboard folder on your desk; it can contain subfolders for organizing files into smaller groups.

Folder name A unique, descriptive name for a folder that helps identify the folder's contents.

Forum An electronic gathering place on the World Wide Web where anyone can add questions and answers on issues; available on the Microsoft Answers website.

Gadget An optional program you can display on your desktop that presents helpful or entertaining information, such as a clock, current news headlines, a calendar, a picture album, or a weather report.

Group In a Microsoft program window's Ribbon, a section containing related command buttons.

Hard disk A built-in, high-capacity, high-speed storage medium for all the software, folders, and files on a computer.

Highlighted Describes the changed appearance of an item or other object, usually a change in its color, background color, and/or border; often used for an object on which you will perform an action, such as a desktop icon.

Homegroup A named group of Windows 7 computers that can share information, including libraries and printers.

Icon A small image, usually on the desktop, which represents items on your computer, such as the Recycle Bin; you can rearrange, add, and delete desktop icons.

Inactive window An open window you are not currently using; if multiple windows are open, the window(s) with the dimmed title bar.

Insertion point In a document or filename, a blinking, vertical bar that indicates where the next character you type will appear.

Keyboard shortcut A key or a combination of keys that you press to perform a command.

Keyword A descriptive word or phrase you enter to obtain a list of results that include that word or phrase.

Library A window that shows files and folders stored in different storage locations; default libraries in Windows 7 include the Documents, Music, Pictures, and Videos libraries.

Link Text or an image that you click to display another location, such as a Help topic, a Web site, or a device.

List box A box that displays a list of options from which you can choose (you may need to scroll and adjust your view to see additional options in the list).

Log in To select a user account name when a computer starts up, giving access to that user's files.

Log off To close all windows, programs, and documents, then display the Welcome screen.

Maximize button On the right side of a window's title bar, the center button of three buttons; use to expand a window so that it fills the entire screen. In a maximized screen, this button turns into a Restore button.

Maximized window A window that fills the desktop.

Menu A list of related commands.

Menu bar A horizontal bar in a window that displays menu names, or categories of related commands.

Microsoft Answers A Microsoft website that lets you search forums, Microsoft Help files, and demonstration videos.

Microsoft Windows 7 An operating system.

Minimize button On the right side of a window's title bar, the left-most button of three buttons; use to reduce a window so that it only appears as an icon on the taskbar.

Minimized window A window that is visible only as an icon on the taskbar.

Mouse pointer A small arrow or other symbol on the screen that you move by manipulating the pointing device; also called a pointer.

Move To change the location of a file, folder, or other object by physically placing it in another location.

Navigate To move around in your computer's folder and file hierarchy.

Navigate downward To move to a lower level in your computer's folder and file hierarchy.

Navigate upward To move to a higher level in your computer's folder and file hierarchy.

Navigation pane A pane on the left side of a window that contains links to folders and libraries on your computer; click an item in the Navigation pane to display its contents in the file list or click the ▷ or ◢ symbols to display or hide subfolders in the Navigation pane.

Notification area An area on the right side of the Windows 7 taskbar that displays the current time as well as icons representing programs; displays pop-up messages when a program on your computer needs your attention.

Operating system A program that manages the complete operation of your computer and lets you interact with it.

Option button A small circle in a dialog box that you click to select only one of two or more related options.

Password A special sequence of numbers and letters known only to selected users, that users can create to control who can access the files in their user account area; helps keep users' computer information secure.

Path The sequence of folders that describes a file location in the file hierarchy; appears in the Address bar of Windows Explorer and the Open and Save dialog boxes.

Point To position the tip of the mouse pointer over an object, option, or item.

Pointer *See* Mouse pointer.

Pointing device A device that lets you interact with your computer by controlling the movement of the mouse pointer on your computer screen; examples include a mouse, trackball, touchpad, pointing stick, on-screen touch pointer, or a tablet.

Pointing device action A movement you execute with your computer's pointing device to communicate with the computer; the five pointing device actions are point, click, double-click, drag, and right click.

Power button 1) The physical button on your computer that turns your computer on. 2) The Start menu button or button on the right side of the Welcome screen that lets you shut down or restart your computer. Click the button arrow to log off your user account, switch to another user, or hibernate the computer to put your computer to sleep so that your computer appears off and uses very little power.

Preview pane A pane on the right side of a window that shows the actual contents of a selected file without opening a program; might not work for some types of files.

Program A set of instructions written for a computer, such as an operating system program or an application program; also called an application.

Program window The window that opens after you start a program, showing you the tools you need to use the program and any open program documents.

Properties Characteristics or settings of a file, folder, or other item, such as its size or the date it was created.

Quick Access toolbar A small toolbar on the left side of a Microsoft application program window's title bar, containing icons that you click to quickly perform common actions, such as saving a file.

RAM (random access memory) The storage location that is part of every computer that temporarily stores open programs and documents information while a computer is on.

Recycle Bin A desktop object that stores folders and files you delete from your hard drive(s) and that enables you to restore them.

Removable storage Storage media that you can easily transfer from one computer to another, such as DVDs, CDs, or USB flash drives.

Restore Down button On the right side of a maximized window's title bar, the center of three buttons; use to reduce a window to its last non-maximized size.

Ribbon In many Microsoft application program windows, a horizontal strip near the top of the window that contains tabs (pages) of grouped command buttons that you click to interact with the program.

Right-click To press and release the right button on the pointing device; use to display a shortcut menu with commands you issue by left-clicking them.

ScreenTip A small box that appears when you position the mouse over an object; identifies the object when you point to it.

Scroll To adjust your view to see portions of the program window that are not currently in a window.

Scroll arrow A button at each end of a scroll bar for adjusting your view in a window in small increments in that direction.

Scroll bar A vertical or horizontal bar that appears along the right or bottom side of a window when there is more content than can be displayed within the window, so that you can adjust your view.

Scroll box A box in a scroll bar that you can drag to display a different part of a window.

Search criteria Descriptive text that helps Windows identify the program, folder, file, or Web site you want to locate.

Select To change the appearance of an item by clicking, double-clicking, or dragging across it, to indicate that you want to perform an action on it.

Select pointer The mouse pointer shape that looks like a white arrow oriented toward the upper-left corner of the screen.

Shortcut An icon that acts as a link to a program, file, folder, or device that you use frequently.

Shortcut menu A menu of context-appropriate commands for an object that opens when you right-click that object.

Shut down To turn off your computer.

Single-click *See* Click.

Slider A shape you drag to select a setting, such as the slider on the View menu that you drag to select a view.

Sort Change the order of, such as the order of files or folders in a window based on criteria such as date, file size, or alphabetical by filename.

Spin box A text box with up and down arrows; you can type a setting in the text box or click the arrows to increase or decrease the setting.

Start button The round button on the left side of the Windows 7 taskbar; click it to start programs, to find and open windows that show you the contents of your computer, to get help, and to end your Windows session, and turn off your computer.

Status bar A horizontal bar at the bottom of a program window that displays simple helpful information and tips.

Subfolder A folder within another folder for organizing sets of related files into smaller groups.

Switch User To lock your user account and display the Welcome screen so another user can log on.

Tab A page in an application program's Ribbon, or in a dialog box, that contains a group of related settings.

Taskbar The horizontal bar at the bottom of the Windows 7 desktop; displays the Start button, the Notification area, and icons representing programs, folders, and/or files.

Text box A box in which you type text, such as the Search programs and files text box on the Start menu.

Title bar The shaded top border of a window that displays the name of the window, folder, or file and the program name. Darker shading indicates the active window.

Toolbar In an application program, a set of buttons you can click to issue program commands.

Touch pointer A pointer on the screen for performing pointing operations with a finger if touch input is available on your computer.

Translucency The transparency feature of Windows Aero that enables you to locate content by seeing through one window to the next window.

USB flash drive (also called a pen drive, flash drive, jump drive, keychain drive, or thumb drive) A removable storage device for folders and files that you plug into a USB port on your computer; makes it easy to transport folders and files to other computers.

User account A special area in a computer's operating system where users can store their own files.

View Appearance choices for your folder contents, such as Large Icons view or Details view.

Welcome screen An initial startup screen that displays icons for each user account on the computer.

Window A rectangular-shaped work area that displays a program or a collection of files, folders, and Windows tools.

Windows Aero *See* Aero.

Windows Explorer An accessory program that displays windows, allowing you to navigate your computer's file hierarchy and interact with your computer's contents.

Windows Remote Assistance A Windows Help feature that lets you connect with another computer so that user can operate your computer using an Internet connection.

Windows Search The Windows feature that lets you look for files and folders on your computer storage devices; to search, type text in the Search text box in the title bar of any open window, or click the Office button and type text in the Search programs and files text box.

Index